Khushwant Singh...

in the name of the father

ISBN: 81-7436-315-7

Published in India by
Roli Books in arrangement
with Roli & Janssen BV
M-75 Greater Kailash-II (Market)
New Delhi 110 048, India.
Phone: 29212271, 29212782
Fax: 29217185
Email: roli@vsnl.com
Website: rolibooks.com

Printed and bound in India

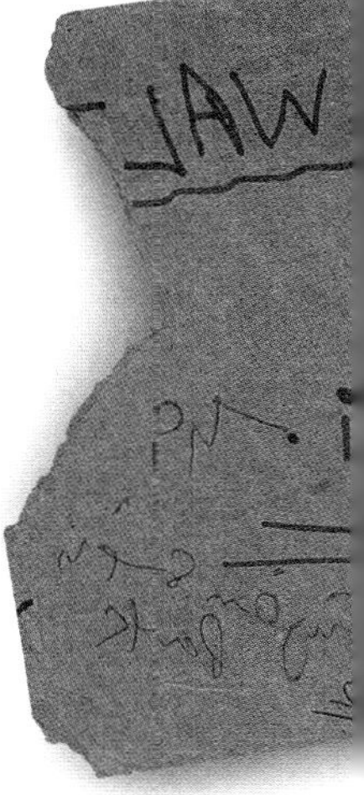

Family Pride

Khushwant Singh

in the name of the father

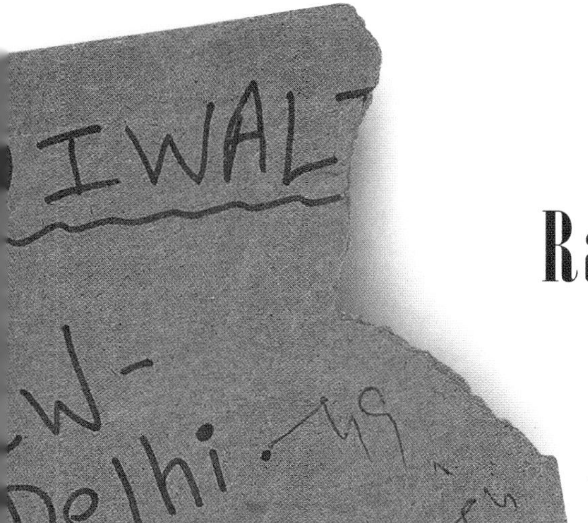

Rahul Singh

Lustre Press
Roli Books

To Alisha Bilimoria,
in the hope that she too
becomes a writer.

PUNJAB
Respected Sh. Khushwant jee,
Namaskar,
Best wishes for the new year (2004)
LAHORE GOVT. COLLEGE
ST. STEPHEN COLLEGE DELHI
KINGS – INNER TEMPLE COLLEGE LONDON
I'M JUST TRYING MY BEST TO KEEP MY BONES AND FLESH TOGETHER.. BUT STILL AWAITING FOR A GOOD OPPORTUNITY.
LAHORE HIGH COURT
EXTERNAL AFFAIRS

Happy New Year

Contents

On a Personal Note

It is difficult enough to write about one's father. It is even more difficult to write about a father like Khushwant Singh. So when Pramod Kapoor of Roli Books asked me whether I would do what he termed 'an archival history' of my father, I was a little mystified and hesitant. As he went on to explain that what he was looking for was an account of my father's life through whatever I could lay my hands on—photographs mainly, but also letters, mementos, news clippings, cartoons, awards, and the like—my doubts began to clear. This would not be a typical biography though it would borrow a great deal from his life and would be profusely illustrated. Instead, this 'archival history' would do what is rarely done in India—trace the story of a remarkable individual's life by highlighting the turning points and influences that shaped it.

We Indians, perhaps, do not have an adequate sense of history. The first authentic accounts of India were given by outsiders like Hiuen Tsang, the Chinese pilgrim, Megasthenes, the Greek historian and diplomat, Marco Polo, the Venetian traveller, and other scholars such as Strabo, Aristoboulos and Onesikritos who followed in the wake of Alexander the Great's invasion of India. Hiuen Tsang travelled to India at the age of twenty-nine (AD 629) and was already considered a Buddhist scholar. He spent several years visiting almost every province of the country, writing down his observations during his travels. After returning to China with a large collection of manuscripts, relics, and images from India, he got together some scholars to compile an exhaustive and authoritative narrative of his journey. 'It is impossible to overestimate the debt which the history of India owes to Hiuen Tsang,' writes Vincent Smith in his definitive *The Oxford History of India*. Megasthenes,

Strabo and Marco Polo, too, left behind exhaustive accounts of their stay in India.

The most objective and authoritative books, for instance, on eminent Indians have largely been written, not by Indians, but foreigners. Louis Fischer's marvellous volume on Mahatma Gandhi and Hugh Toye's equally engaging account of Netaji Subhash Chandra Bose's life immediately come to mind.

Though later in life my father became something of a historian himself, he kept very few records of himself and his life, especially of his early life. As a result, the reader will inevitably find a bit about my life in this book—one of my means to illustrate some of my father's traits and his worldview.

From Hadali to Delhi

1

I am sure that if the mothers of various nations could meet, there would be no more wars.

— E.M. Forster

My father was born in 1915 in Hadali. Located in the Thal desert, and close to the Jhelum river, Hadali is located in what is today Pakistan. Around the time when my father was born, the village had some three hundred families, mostly Baluchis. Strangely, his father Sobha Singh and his grandfather Sujan Singh, were away in Delhi at the time and did not bother to rush back to the village at the news of the birth. Business was clearly more important than the birth of a grandson or a son, especially a second one at that. What is more, there was no record of the time of the birth. Sobha Singh made no mention of it in his diary, and villages in those days maintained no records of births and deaths. Also, unlike Hindus, since most Sikhs did not believe either in astrology or in casting horoscopes, for which the precise time and exact location of birth are considered essential, there was little reason to have bothered recording either. It was only several years later, when Sobha Singh had to get his eldest two sons (there were eventually to be four sons, and a daughter), admitted to Delhi's Modern School, that he had to cook up a couple of dates of birth. For my father he chose 2 February 1915. Much later, my father's grandmother told my father that he had been born in *Badroo*, which is August. So, he decided on

FACING PAGE:

Sir Sobha Singh with his family.

My grandparents are seated with their children around them. At the top extreme right is my father.

August 15, which, by sheer happenstance, was to become the day India would gain independence. So, my father has two birthdays, six months apart, neither of which is his real birthday!

Quite soon after my father's birth, Sobha Singh took his wife and elder son to Delhi, where he had to attend to some building contracts. My father was left behind for the first few years of his life in the care of his grandmother, Lakshmi Bai, for whom he developed a strong attachment. His memories of Hadali are hazy, as he had moved to Delhi quite early in life. But he would return to Hadali thrice: the first time to read the *Japji*—the Sikh morning prayer—aloud to a gathering; the second time, while practising Law in Lahore; the third and most memorable occasion was in 1987, during a visit to Pakistan. There were no more Hindus or Sikhs left in Hadali but the two thousand Muslims villagers had welcomed him as one of their own. Moved by the

gesture he had broken down while addressing them. There was a display of fireworks as he was escorted to his ancestral home, which had been festooned with balloons and colourful streamers. He was pleasantly surprised to discover that the Hindu-Sikh dharmasala which had been a place of worship, had been left untouched by the Muslims.

The Partition of India in 1947 was traumatic for my parents' generation, for all those Indians who happened to be living in what was to later become Pakistan, and for those Pakistanis living in what would soon be India. An overwhelming majority of Hindus and Sikhs were compelled to leave their homes in Pakistan, often amidst violence and bloodshed, and became refugees overnight. Embittered by the experience and filled with hatred, many of them became anti-Muslim and anti-Pakistan. Not my father though. He said that blood was spilt on both sides. Hindus and Sikhs butchered Muslims, and Muslims butchered Hindus and Sikhs. He even saw one of his own students being killed and felt that some kind of mad frenzy had taken hold of all the communities. Forced to abandon his home in Lahore and a successful law practice, he too became a refugee and left the city with more sorrow and regret than bitterness.

He tried his best to keep in touch with his Muslim friends in Pakistan, but that was not easy. An iron curtain seemed to have come down between India and Pakistan. On the mantlepiece in my father's room in his flat in Sujan Singh Park, a photograph of him, my mother and a couple has occupied a prominent place for as long as I can remember. The couple are Asghari and Manzur Qadir, amongst his dearest friends, and whom I think he missed the most after the tragic turn of events in 1947.

Manzur, a prominent lawyer, served as Pakistan's Foreign Minister in the military government of Ayub Khan.

FACING PAGE:

My parents with Manzur and Asghari Qadir

This photograph has been in the living room of the Sujan Singh house for as long as I can remember. Manzur, a prominent lawyer in Lahore who went on to become Pakistan's Foreign Minister under President Ayub Khan, was my father's closest friend in Lahore. The friendship with the couple continued after Partition and, I believe, is one of the main reasons why my father, despite the trauma of Partition, remains fundamentally pro-Muslim and an ardent proponent of close Indo-Pak relations.

The daughter of the Qadirs, Shirin, went to Cambridge University in England at the same time as I did. She became a very close friend of mine, so the family friendship continued over another generation. When she married Khalid Ikram (who was also at Cambridge the same time as we were) in Lahore in 1963, my mother and I went to Pakistan to attend the wedding.

It was my first visit to Pakistan after Partition and I was cautioned against it as I was taking my entrance exams for the Indian Administrative Service (IAS). 'It will go against you when the final selection is made,' I was advised. I went to my father to find out what he had to say on the matter. He said, 'Go ahead. Never mind what others have to say, friendship must come first.' At that time, he loved quoting E.M. Forster from *Two Cheers for Democracy*: '...if I had to choose between betraying my country and betraying my friend, I hope I should have the guts to betray my country.' To date it remains a favourite quote with my father.

Taking a cue from it, I opted for the friend and went to Lahore for the wedding. Manzur Qadir took me to Islamabad, the capital of Pakistan, as well as to Lyallpur, where he was to present a convocation address, and from there to Murree, a hill station.

Though I did well in my written exams for the IAS, I did not fare too well in the interview. I was asked about the origin of my name, Rahul, to which I answered correctly — it was the name of Gautam Buddha's son. But when I was quizzed on Buddhism, I may have floundered, having mostly done modern European history and political theory at Cambridge! The upshot was that I did not get into the IAS, to the disappointment, I think, of my father.

Taya Zinkin, a well-known journalist who had written several books on India and had been the correspondent in

India for the prestigious and well-known British daily newspaper, *The Manchester Guardian*, wrote in one of her books on India that I did not manage to make it to the IAS because I had been foolish enough to go to Pakistan at that juncture and was presumably therefore considered a security risk. I still do not know if that was the truth.

After the IAS 'debacle' I was offered fairly lucrative jobs in the corporate sector, but I turned them down.

'You might regret it one day,' my father said.

I didn't and still don't. Instead I took to journalism, quite a few of my articles having appeared in university publications in England, as well as in *The Illustrated Weekly of India* and *The Sunday Standard*. My father was a close friend of Evan Charlton, the editor of *The Statesman* in Delhi. Charlton gave me some reporting assignments. I was also asked by my father to meet S. Mulgaonkar, the legendary editor of *The Hindustan Times*, Delhi's leading daily newspaper, as well as Sham Lal, the resident editor of *The Times of India* in Delhi. I worked for a few months as a trainee with *The Hindustan Times* but eventually *The Times of India* made me the best offer—an assistant editor, straightaway—though that meant moving to Bombay.

'I shall pay for a month's stay at a modest but centrally located hotel for you,' my father told me. 'After that, you must manage on your own.'

This personal aside is only meant to show how much friendship—and all that friendship implies—meant and still means to my father. Friendship was more important than even love for one's country. I also realized that he believed that children must learn to stand on their own feet, as soon as their education is over. The parents' duty and economic support ends at that point, he felt. It was a very Western notion, since in India sometimes children tend to be dependent on their parents well into adulthood—something that my father was dead against.

When I joined *The Times of India* my monthly salary was less than Rs 500, but I was able to find a nice paying guest accommodation with breakfast for half that amount with a lovely Parsi couple, Ami and Firdaus Jehangir. A Royal Enfield motorcycle that my grandfather had presented me in Delhi was sent to me by rail to Bombay. I was on my own and managed fairly comfortably. The only financial help I got from home was the occasional bottle of rum!

To set the record straight, I should also add here that I became a journalist much before my father did if one were to discount his stint with *Yojana*, but more about that later. Most people imagine that I followed in my father's footsteps, whereas it was actually the other way round. I had already done a five-year stint as assistant editor of *The Times of India* before he became editor of *The Illustrated Weekly of India*.

Coming back to Partition and my father's friendship with the Qadirs, even in India he has always gone out of his way to befriend Muslims, and kept his distance from those he finds communally biased, be that against Muslims or practitioners of other faiths. He has also been constantly and vociferously pro-Pakistani, convinced that more people-to-people ties, rather than confrontation, would lead to better relations between the two nations. Whenever he goes to Pakistan, he is warmly received and is probably just as well known in Pakistan as in India. Visiting writers, poets and artistes from Pakistan make it a point to call on him. His doors have always been open to them, even when relations between the two countries have been at their worst.

World War I saw an upturn in the family's fortunes. The British government gifted my great-grandfather, Sujan Singh, large tracts of land for having helped recruit soldiers for the army and for giving donations in cash for the war. My grand-uncle, Ujjal Singh, was put in charge of these lands and the cotton ginning and spinning mills that were set up there. Ujjal Singh, incidentally, was the first person in the family to go to college and get a Master's degree. Later in life, he went on to become a minister in the Punjab government, and Governor of Punjab and Tamil Nadu as well. His brother who was my grandfather, on the other hand, was relatively unlettered and not as sophisticated. But he had a head for business.

Sobha Singh's first venture, however, was not a success. He decided to buy an ailing cotton mill near Subzi Mandi in Delhi, which he renamed Khalsa Cotton Spinning and Weaving Mills. At this point my father and his grandmother were shifted from Hadali to Delhi. My father must have been about five or six. Meanwhile, his mother had given birth to another son and a daughter. Hence my father had three brothers and a sister. The cotton mill venture was a business disaster that almost plunged the family into bankruptcy. Sobha Singh must have realized that his real talent lay in constructing buildings. New Delhi was then being planned and large areas were being sold to contractors. Sobha Singh purchased a large chunk at an almost throwaway price. Some of that land would later become a large part of what is now Connaught Place, the prime shopping area of New Delhi, with the highest real estate prices in the city.

School and College

2

I rejoice in my spine, as in the firm audacious staff of that flag which I fling half out to the world.

— Herman Melville

It was around this time that my father entered school. Sobha Singh's choice of school for his eldest two sons was an unusual but inspired one, indicating his nationalist leanings. The school had been founded by Lala Raghubir Singh who had a wealthy father in Rai Bahadur Lala Sultan Singh. Instead of turning to business like his father, Lala Raghubir Singh decided on education. Thus was born the now famous Modern School. Unlike the better-known English-style public schools such as Doon School and Mayo College, the emphasis in Modern School was on patriotism, combined with the best that the West had to offer. Though English was the medium of instruction, Sanskrit, Hindi and Urdu were taught as well. Students were made to feel proud of their culture and tradition.

Modern School was a radical departure from the schools of the past in another respect—it was the first co-educational school in Delhi. Amongst those studying in Modern School with my father, was Kaval Malik, a year younger than him. She would become his wife almost twenty years later. My father spent ten years at Modern School. Though he was not too good either at studies or at games, he developed a love for Urdu poetry and for the English language—a rather strange combination. The two loves have endured all his life. He also

FACING PAGE:

A school with a difference.

Modern School in those days was known to lay stress on Indian culture and tradition. Hence it was to Modern School that Sir Sobha Singh sent his two eldest sons.

SATURDAY, AUGUST 26, 1950.

INDIAN AUTHOR COMPARED WITH TOLSTOY: "THE MARK OF VISHNU"

THERE HAVE been rare occasions when a work of fiction, often quite a modest one, has epitomised a new era in a nation's development. In some way it has caught and fixed a characteristic feature, and in a flash illuminated a period.

Such a book, from what must appear a most unlikely source, is **The Mark of Vishnu**, by Khushwant Singh, Press Attache at India House, recently published here by the Saturn Press. It is a collection of short stories, some serious, and some very funny indeed, dealing with Indians in their own country and abroad.

★

The book has had a remarkable success here, particularly for an Indian author, and received the highest praise from such papers as **The Times Literary Supplement, The Observer** and **The Manchester Guardian.** The latter even finds it reminiscent of Tolstoy.

To me it rather recalled Maupassant in its skilled handling of language, and the way in which the author in a few deft sentences sketches not only atmosphere and character, but an idea, often only suggested, that lingers on like a fragrance after the sentence is finished. I have never before seen the English language so subtly treated by an Indian. Maupassant set a standard seldom achieved by short-story writers, though many have tried. This one has hit a bull's-eye without apparently trying at all.

★

But more important is the fact that probably quite without intention or even full awareness on the author's part, the book portrays the great psychological change that has overtaken Indians since they achieved nationhood.

KHUSHWANT SINGH

. . . Author of "The Mark of Vishnu"

There is here none of the aggressiveness that really covers a painful feeling of inferiority, nor of the uncertainty and the obscurantism that so often mar the writings of Indians. There are plenty of sly digs at Europeans and Americans, but above all there is a quality new, I think, in Indian writers, which enables the author to bare his own weaknesses with detachment, and poke fun at himself both as an individual and as an Indian.

In a new way he makes Indians intelligible to Europeans because he regards them at one and the same time with inner understanding, from an Indian's eye view, as it were, and from without, with the point of view of the sophisticated European. I look forward to a work on a larger canvas from this author.

—PAULA WIKING.

loved playing pranks, some of which got him into trouble. One of them clearly bordered on the dangerous.

Having found a cobra in the garden, my father and his brothers smashed it to pulp but left the head intact. Taking it to be dead, they put it into a biscuit tin, fastened the lid securely with a string, and presented the tin to their chemistry teacher who had a variety of snakes in methylated spirit in jars, but no cobra. The teacher got a jar of methylated spirit, untied the string of the lid, and put his hand in the tin to take out what he imagined was a dead cobra. Instead a live and angrily hissing cobra sprang out, its deadly fangs just missing the startled teacher's face. That incident would later be turned into one of my father's best short stories, *The Mark of Vishnu*, which was published by *Harper's Magazine*, a prestigious American publication.

My father's Modern School days (1920–30) coincided with a change in Sobha Singh's fortunes. Realizing that he may not be successful with textiles, he decided to concentrate on what he was really good at—making

AIR MAIL

ALL INDIA RADIO
GOVERNMENT OF INDIA

TELEGRAMS AIRVOICE
TELEPHONE 31031 (4 lines.)

101, Queen's Road,
BOMBAY.

Ref. No. DE-S

Date 6th Dec.'50

My dear Khushwant,

I am herewith enclosing a royalty contract form for the broadcast of your story 'The Mark of Vishnu'. It is scheduled on the 27th of March 1951 from 10 to 10.30 P.M. and is being adopted for the radio by a member of our staff, Mr. Adi Marzban. As soon as the script is finalised I shall let you have a copy. Would you be good enough to sign this contract at a very early date and send it by return of post ?

I am also enclosing extracts from a book review broadcast on the 13th November '50 which included a review of your book 'The Mark of Vishnu'. The talk was broadcast by Mr. R.MacC. Samples of the British Information Service.

I hope you are well.

With kind regards,

Yours sincerely,

(N.Iqbal Singh)

Khushwant Singh, Esq.
Public Relations Officer
to Indian High Commissioner,
India House,
London.

PUBLIC RELATIONS
DEPARTMENT
11 DEC 1950
2 013364

Encl: 1 contract
1 extract

buildings. He landed the contract to build the South Block. Temporarily, he shifted his residence to what is now Rafi Marg, and was then called Old Mill Road because of a flourmill there. A railway track had been laid there to facilitate transporting building materials from Badarpur (now full of fashionable farmhouses), some 18 kilometres away, to where North and South Blocks, along with Parliament House and Rashtrapati Bhawan, were to come up. As the construction work gathered pace, my grandfather bought a three-acre plot on Jantar Mantar road and built a double-storeyed house, with clerks' and servants' quarters, buffalo sheds, stables for horses, a tennis court and a huge garden in which he could indulge a passion he had developed: growing flowers, especially roses. He named the house Baikunth (paradise). It was later sold to the Maharaja of Travancore, and is today the Guest House of the Kerala State Government. Later my grandfather built a grander house on what is now 1A Janpath, opposite Claridges Hotel. That house is presently leased to the Hungarian Embassy.

It was during my father's Modern School days that he became aware of his first sexual stirrings. Once when he was seriously ill and barely conscious, he recalls the nurse who was attending to him, fondling him in an intimate manner and making him touch her breasts.

With schooling at Modern School over, my father applied for admission to Delhi's St. Stephen's College, then as now, probably the most prestigious college in India. He escaped the traditional ragging because he came down with typhoid. After two relapses, the doctors told his family to be prepared for the worst. His grandmother came over to see if she could somehow improve his condition. Her treatment consisted of tying a coloured string on the big toe of his left foot and chanting from the *Guru Granth Sahib* day and night. Miraculously, as it were, my father's condition improved.

At this point I should add that in the last couple of years, he has developed a fondness for listening to the sacred Sikh hymns aired on TV from the Golden Temple at Amritsar, early in the morning and in the evening. My sister and I poke fun at this pastime of his, since he has always claimed to be a non-believer. Perhaps, it is a throwback to his early days, especially to the time when he was cured from typhoid by his grandmother's devotion. Anyway, he was sent to the hills, to Simla to convalesce. There he fell in love with the Himalayas, a love that has since endured, and also began to write poetry.

Around the time of his return to St. Stephen's College, in his second year, the three revolutionaries, Bhagat Singh, Raj Guru and Sukhdev were hanged by the British authorities. My grandfather, Sobha Singh, through no fault of his, got tangled up with the prosecution of Bhagat Singh.

Sobha Singh happened to be sitting in the Visitors' Gallery of the Legislative Assembly in New Delhi, when Bhagat Singh threw a bomb from that very Gallery on the legislators below. In fact, at the very time Bhagat Singh was about to hurl the bomb, my grandfather had taken his seat at one end of the Gallery and was looking for some friends whom he had planned to meet for lunch, and who were sitting at the other end of the Gallery. By sheer chance, they were sitting just behind Bhagat Singh and his associate, Batukeshwar Dutt. The moment Bhagat Singh hurled the bomb my grandfather spotted his friends—and, needless to say, saw the bomb being hurled. He was asked to appear as a witness for prosecution, which he did. There were other witnesses as well but since he was already a well-known and respected figure, the British authorities felt that his testimony as a witness would have greater impact on the judge who was trying the case.

It later came to light that the bomb had made to injure, not kill. Bhagat Singh and Dutt's intention was to commit a symbolic act of defiance. However, Bhagat Singh had earlier shot and killed a policeman, Saunders. But no evidence could link him to the crime. After the bomb attack, the British authorities were able to establish that Bhagat Singh was the person who had killed Saunders. Bhagat Singh was hanged, not for the bomb thrown in the Legislative Assembly, but for the murder of Saunders.

Years later, in 1997, after my grandfather was long gone, public attention was drawn to this incident somewhat mischievously, by a news item in *The Indian Express*. 'Khushwant Singh's Father was Main Witness in Bhagat Singh's Trial', read the sensational headline. The innuendo in the news item was that my grandfather had somehow collaborated with the British to prosecute and eventually hang Bhagat Singh, a completely erroneous and politically motivated interpretation.

The person dragged into the controversy that followed, was actually my father, by then a prominent and influential public figure. The idea was to show that he came from an anti-national, traitorous family! Even I received an anonymous threatening phone call in Bombay, and some hate mail soon after the story had been published. A gentleman called M.S. Kilpady, a contributor to *Kanara Sarawat*, sent me a letter accusing me of being a Sangh Parivar hate-monger and challenging me to include this incident about my grandfather's role in the Bhagat Singh trial in this book. The irony of course is that Bhagat Singh, after hurling his bomb in the legislative Assembly, had no intention of even trying to escape. He and Dutt wanted to

defy the British by this symbolic act of defiance and gave themselves up to the British authorities straightaway. The other irony is that the Jan Sangh, or the Sangh Parivar for that matter, hardly played any role in the independence movement, and Bhagat Singh, with his leftist ideology, was far removed from the Jan Sangh and the Hindu Mahasabha.

My father's years in St Stephen's College were quite uneventful. Having spent too much time playing tennis, he did not do particularly well in his studies, and just

With Balraj Sahni

Balraj was a friend of my father from their early pre-Partition Lahore days. Balraj was passionate about the Punjabi language and had one of the earliest Gurmukhi typewriters.

about managed to clear his Intermediate Arts exams. Even in tennis, he could not get into the college B team. His parents were in a dilemma over what was to be done with him. Since he was talkative and argumentative, they felt that he was cut out to be a lawyer. So, it was Government College, Lahore, which was just as well known and prestigious as St. Stephen's College. However, there too, he fared no better academically. Instead he became friends with students who would later become household names from the film industry. Amongst them was Balraj Sahni, (the hero of *Do Bigha Zameen* and *Garam Hawa*), Chetan Anand (the director of *Haqeeqat*, and Dev Anand's brother), and B.R. Chopra, the maker of memorable films.

After one of his trips to Pakistan, my father wrote three articles for *The Times of India*. My father's friend, Manzur Qadir, was then the foreign minister of Pakistan, Ayub Khan the president and Zulifikar Ali Bhutto a minister. The articles, by and large, praised the Pakistani regime for being both modern and run by relatively young people. Balraj Sahni clearly did not like the articles.

'I pay ten paise to read how handsome and well-dressed Pakistani ministers are,' he told my father sarcastically.

'You only pay ten paise,' my father retorted. 'I pay five rupees to see you dancing the flamenco!' My father was obviously referring to one of his lesser films.

My father visited Balraj Sahni a few times after the actor had settled down in Bombay. He recalls how Balraj Sahni wrote all his letters in Gurmukhi and possessed one of the first Gurmukhi typewriters. Proud of his language, he wanted dearly to promote it, both in India and Pakistan. My father also noticed that in his study lay a copy of the *Guru Granth Sahib* which Balraj Sahini said he consulted all the time.

Chetan Anand and B.R. Chopra were in my father's class, while Dev Anand was a junior in school. Kamini Kaushal was also a contemporary of my father and very close to my parents. Of all these people Chetan Anand, says my father, became his closest friend and would often stay with him in Lahore. But my father concluded that Chetan was 'self-centred' and a 'fabricator'. Chetan claimed that he had written the script of the *Son-et-Lumière* at the Red Fort. When my father, the real script-writer, confronted him, Chetan admitted that he had actually lied. 'In the nine years that I lived in Bombay,' says my father, 'Chetan did not invite me over to his house even once.'

With Shashi and Jennifer Kapoor

Shashi Kapoor had agreed to finance and act as the male lead in a proposed Merchant-Ivory production of my father's novel Train to Pakistan. *But somehow the project fell through.*

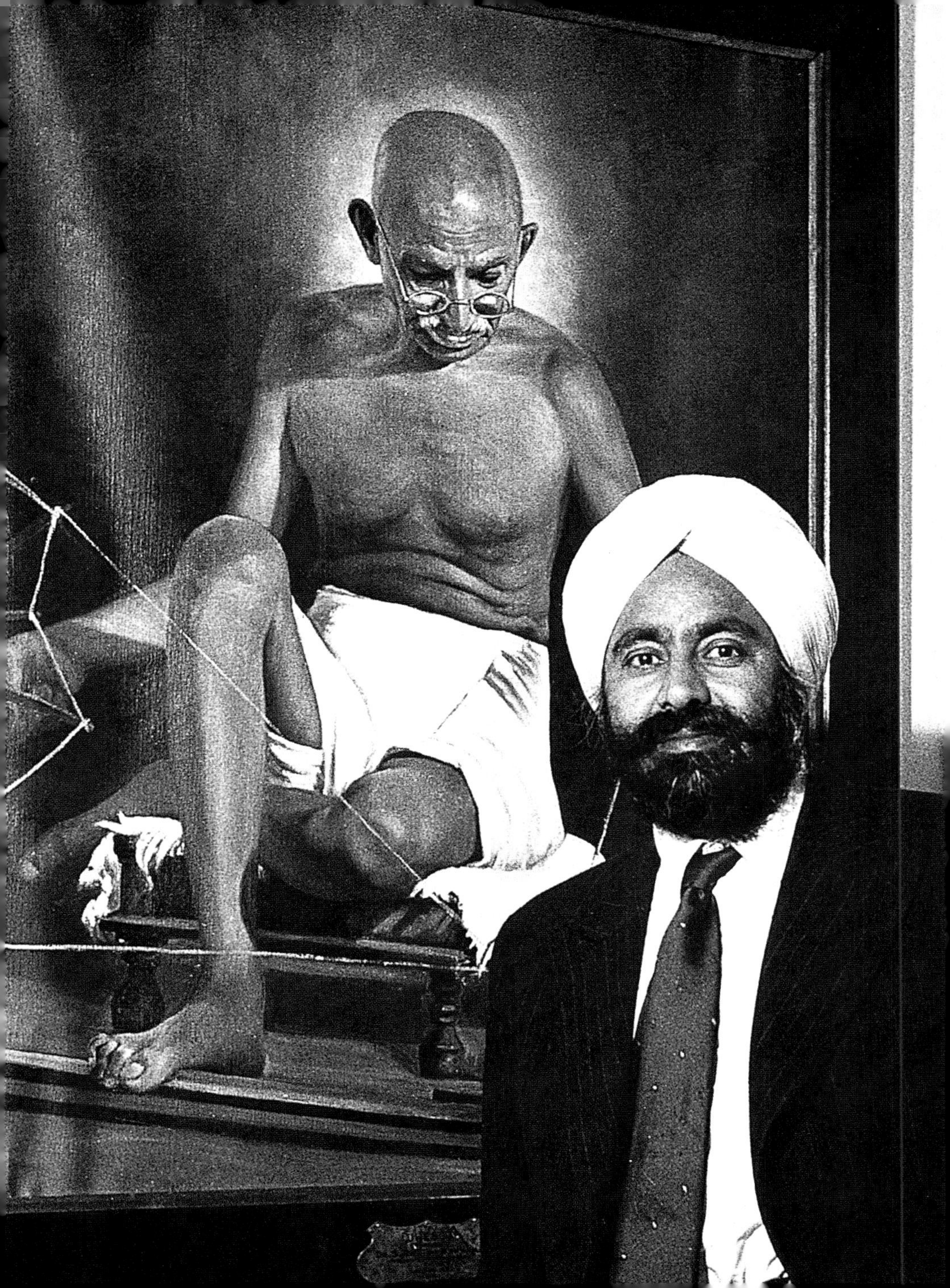

Westward Bound and an Engagement

3

Wherever you go,
go with all your heart.

—Confucius

My father's Government College days were punctuated by an interesting interlude. During the first summer vacation, he decided to find out if his aptitude lay in the arts. The best-known place for this was the Vishwabharati University at Shantiniketan in West Bengal, not very far from Calcutta. With a letter of recommendation from a Bengali friend, Ashok Sen, whose father owned some land at Shantiniketan, my father managed to get admission. Soon, however, he realized that he was not cut out to be a painter, though he did learn to play the sitar fairly well. His sojourn at Shantiniketan came to an end in a curious fashion: the mosquitoes there made his life miserable and the doctor, seeing his plight, told him to pack his bags and leave as soon as possible. So back to Government College he came where he managed to get just a Bachelor's degree, with a third division. Neither Oxford nor Cambridge University would admit anyone with a third division. So, the choice fell on King's College, London University, where he enrolled for an L.L.B. while applying for admission to the Inner Temple to qualify as a barrister. In those days like most other students, he took a ship from India to England.

The two passengers with whom he struck up a

FACING PAGE:

Next to a portrait of Mahatma Gandhi.

My father had unstinting admiration for a few people. Gandhi was one of them, the other one being Mother Teresa.

Tennis champion.

My father enrolled for an L.L.B. at King's College , London, and distinguished himself more on the tennis courts than in academics.

Club, 1st Team, 1937.
INTER-COLLEGIATE COMPETITION.

friendship on that journey were Somnath Chib, who had recently been appointed a lecturer at Dayal Singh College, Lahore, and would later become India's first Director General of Tourism, and Lakshmi Kant Jha, who would become a member of the Indian Civil Service and later serve as Governor of the Reserve Bank of India, and India's Ambassador to the United States. Somnath Chib was honeymooning with his bride, Savitri. My father recalls how the two could not stop kissing each other in front of all the passengers. L.K. Jha, it seems, could not keep his hands to himself when he saw a pretty girl!

London was a dream city. He loved the monuments, the streets, the shop windows, and of course, the women. For his first summer holidays, he decided to return to India, by ship again. Nothing very eventful happened in the two months that he was in India. But just before going back to England, near the neo-Gothic Victoria Terminus (still popularly known as VT but now officially called Chhatrapati Shivaji Station), he lost his virginity in not too glamorous or romantic a manner. He visited a prostitute and paid Rs 10 for the act. Clearly he was disappointed. During the passage to England, he repeatedly examined his penis to check if he had, by any chance, contracted a venereal disease!

His return to London University was marked by a significant event in his life. Teja Singh Malik, a senior engineer (he was later knighted by the British) and his wife, Raj, came to England with their son, Shubchintan (we got to know him as Shubji). They wanted him to pursue agricultural studies at Kent. The other purpose of their visit was to find a suitable match for their daughter, Kaval, who had grown into a ravishing beauty. As orthodox Sikhs, they were keen only on a Sikh for their daughter.

Their first choice was Tarlok Singh who had made it to

the ICS, but since Tarlok Singh was already committed to marrying someone else, they decided to meet other Sikh students in England. My father was completely bowled over by Kaval and set out to woo her. Her parents were lukewarm towards him, mainly because Sobha Singh was a contractor who sought favours from Teja Singh Malik, an engineer. Things changed for my father, however, when Raj Malik, a very devout woman, visited my father's room, and discovered a book of Sikh prayers under his pillow!

Soon after, my father proposed to Kaval and she accepted. Her parents consented to the match. So, my father and Kaval became more or less officially engaged, much to the disappointment of her many suitors, including Pratap Chandra Lal (later the Air Chief Marshal of the Indian Air Force and then the general manager of Indian Airlines) and Bharat Ram, who had been with Kaval in college and was the son of one of India's leading industrialists. Though Bharat Ram was already married, he continued to be interested in Kaval.

My parents' engagement was not a smooth one. He liked to go skiing and this seemed to annoy Kaval. The two of them corresponded with each other but the ardour of their courtship was somehow missing in the correspondence. My father says that my mother used to be quite bored with the letters he wrote her because he did not write about her and she felt left out. He recalls with amusement how she wrote to him from Germany, where she had gone with Bharat Ram, that there was 'somebody called Adolf Hitler who was very popular' and who seemed an admirable person. Then, for about six to eight months, my father and mother drifted apart. They even stopped writing to each other. Both thought the engagement was over. Then one fine day, they made up their minds about spending their lives together.

Life in Lahore

4

Liberty is worth paying for...

—Jules Verne

My father also decided to take a shot at the ICS exams. Though he scored very well in the interview, his written exams let him down (I was to have an entirely different experience: I did well in the written exams and bowed out in the interview). So he narrowly missed making it. And since he did poorly in his L.L.B., there was no question of pursuing a higher law degree. Hence, he returned to India and decided to set up law practice in Lahore where his father had got him a two-bedroom flat. The question of the flagging engagement had to be resolved soon as word had got around that his engagement to Kaval was going to be called off. After the two had discussed the matter, they agreed to sort out their differences and go ahead with the marriage. My father married my mother on 30 October 1939 in the traditional Sikh way in New Delhi.

That evening, my grandfather, Sobha Singh, who had by then acquired quite a name for his lavish parties and generosity, invited over 1,000 guests for dinner and a dance party on the lawns of his house. Amongst the guests was Mohammad Ali Jinnah, the founding father of Pakistan, and who at the time, lived next door. Mohammad Ali Jinnah used to live where the Netherlands Embassy is located today, just across the road from where my grandfather lived. Jinnah used to often visit my grandfather to admire the rose garden of which my grandfather was inordinately proud. Mahatma Gandhi used to stay in Birla House a few minutes

FACING PAGE:
A life together.
This photograph was taken shortly after my parents' wedding.

SIKH WEDDING

MISS K. MALIK AND SARDAR KHUSWANT SINGH

The marriage took place in New Delhi on Monday of Miss Kaval Malik, the eldest daughter of Sardar Bahadur Teja Singh Malik to Sardar Khuswant Singh, the son of Sardar Bahadur Sardar Sobha Singh.

The reception of the bridegroom's party was held on Sunday night, a large number of people, including Mr M. A. Jinnah and Sir Jwahar Singh, attending the function.

The marriage ceremony was performed on Monday morning according to Sikh rites and was largely attended. The bride, who was dressed in a pink costume, looked very pretty. During the ceremony a telegram was received by the bride from her uncle Sardar T. S. Malik, I.C.S., who is Trade Commissioner for India in America.

In the evening the bride's father gave a garden party which was attended by over 500 persons. In a *shamiana* were displayed the numerous presents received by the bride, including a beautiful diamond and pearl set from Sardar Bahadur and Sardarni Sobha Singh

Among those who sent presents were Sir G. V. and Lady Bewoor, Sir A. J. and Lady Raisman, Major-Gen. and Mrs. Tabuteau, Mr. and Mrs. F. T. Jones, Sir Brojendra and Lady Mitter, Mr. and Mrs. Dow, Mr. and Mrs. J. A. Thorne, Mr. and Mrs. A. W. Dean, Mr. and Mrs. Harry Gill, Mr. and Mrs. N. R. Pillai, Mr. and Mrs. B. J. Kirchner, Mr. and Mrs. Webb-Johnson, Mr. and Mrs. F. Tymms, Major and Mrs. Shah, Sir Girja and Lady Bajpai, Sir Maurice Gwyer, Mr. and Mrs. Hume, Mr. and Miss Mitchell, Col. and Mrs. Marsden, Mr. and Mrs. E. S. Lewis, Mr. and Mrs. R. K. Nehru and Mr. Badrul Islam.

The bride was educated in St. Stephen's College, Delhi, and in England; the bridegroom is a barrister.

Those who attended the garden party included Mr. E. M. Jenkins, Chief Commissioner, members of the Viceroy's Executive Council, a large number of Government officials and prominent business men. Statesman Oct 3

away from my grandfather's house. So, Gandhi and Jinnah met a few times at my grandfather's 'middle path' house.

Coming back to the marriage, my parents honeymooned in Mount Abu, famous for its Jain temples. After the honeymoon, my father was back to the grind of being a lawyer in Lahore.

Sadly, my father was not successful in the profession that he had chosen to pursue. In fact he may well have been a dismal failure. For the first few months he did not get a single case to handle, and spent much of his time at the two elite clubs of Lahore, the Cosmopolitan and the Gymkhana, playing tennis and socializing. His father, by then a very wealthy man, subsidized him heavily.

In desperation, my father took on part-time teaching at the Law College and managed to get himself enlisted on the panel of the defence lawyers at the High Court. Since he was something of a Marxist, he defended the cases of communists free of charge. As a result, his earnings never crossed more than a thousand rupees a month. His expenses though were several times that figure. Nonetheless, he continued to practise Law for seven years, but the experience left a bitter taste in his mouth.

In an interview he gave to Pavan K. Varma, diplomat and writer, he explained why he disliked Law as a profession: 'I had a board outside. Very impressive in three languages—Punjabi, Urdu and English: L.L.B., Barrister at Law. I had a clerk and the usual paraphernalia that lawyers have such as a black coat and gown. But there were no clients! They didn't walk in. In Lahore at that time, the

MAN, MONDAY, NOVEMBER 6, 1939.

SIKH WEDDING IN DELHI

Sardar Khuswant Singh, son of Sardar [illegible]adur Sobha Singh, photographed with his bride, Bibi Kaval, daught[illegible] of Sardar Bahadur Teja Singh Malik after their wed[illegible]ng in Delhi.

Newspaper clippings of my parents' wedding.

Last-minute advice.
My mother with some of her close relatives during a special ceremony on the day of her wedding.

entire legal profession—and I think particularly the criminal side—was in the hands of touts. They picked up clients at railway stations and bus stops and went to the villages and brought them. And they took a big cut from the fees you got. Of course, this is strictly immoral and not allowed in the legal profession, but just about everyone had to do it. And then it dawned on me that one had to live. And to make your livelihood on other people's quarrels was something wrong. You owed life more. I would no doubt have improved my practice. It was picking up. I almost certainly would have been a judge at the High Court, if not higher, because people much worse than me got on to the Supreme Court. Of that I had no doubt in my mind. But I did feel a sense of frustration following a profession that did not give me fulfillment.'

His poor opinion of lawyers, and of the judicial system in India, remained with him for a long time. He even ran into trouble for having expressed his opinion on the judiciary in an article that had appeared in *The Hindustan Times*. The subject was corruption in the judiciary. My father was accused of contempt of court in both the Chandigarh High Court and the Allahabad High Court. Siddhartha Shankar Ray appeared in court for my father. My father was told that telling the truth was not a legal defence for what he had written, and was given two days to think his options over—go to jail or apologize. He did the latter though I do not think he changed his view of the judiciary.

The great lawyer, Nani Palkhivala, once said that we have too many laws in India, not enough justice. Also, that a great many Indian judges were corrupt or could be politically influenced. This was true when my father was a lawyer in his twenties, and may well hold true even today.

My father may have been disillusioned with life as a lawyer in Lahore, but he found plenty of time to read good literature and poetry, as well as make lasting friends of the kind that he had not made in Delhi and London. These friends included Manzur and Asghari Qadir, Usha and Wilburn Lal, Justice Gopal Das Khosla and his wife, Shakuntala, Inder Mohan Varma, Bhabhesh Chandra Sanyal, Arthur and Sheila Lal, Prem Kirpal, and E.N. Mangat Rai and his wife, Champa. Most of them, along with their children, became my friends as well (the Rais had no children and Prem Kirpal, now ninety-four years old, remains a bachelor).

One of the sons of the Khoslas, Romi, studied with me at Cambridge University and went on to become one of India's best-known architects. He remains one of my closest friends. Usha and Wilburn Lal's daughter, Premila ('Kinna'), was in

college with me. She was one of Delhi's most popular and attractive girls, with a string of suitors. Behind her back, she was called 'busty Lal' because of her lovely figure, which she displayed to good effect on the tennis courts (she was ranked amongst the top three Indian women players). She broke many hearts, including that of artist M.F. Hussain, and eventually married an Englishman, Charles Lewis, who became head of the Oxford University Press in India. During the Emergency (1975-77), she organized farm labourers on the outskirts of Delhi and led agitations to procure better

wages for them. Unfortunately for her, one of the farms belonged to Mrs Indira Gandhi. Premila paid a price for her activism by spending some time in jail, and was released only after her parents had intervened and she had apologized. She wrote a moving book, *Reason Wounded*, based on this experience.

Arthur Lal was a diplomat posted to various countries. I grew up with his and Sheila Lal's only child, Tookie, a thoroughly spoilt brat, pampered with fancy cars at a very young age. Tragically, she died of cancer while still in her

TOP AND FACING PAGE:
Taking marital vows before the *Guru Granth Sahib*.
My parents almost called off their engagement at a certain point in time before deciding one fine day to let bygones be bygones, and tie the knot.

FACING PAGE::

The newly weds.

The newly wed couple seeking the blessings of the elders for a happy married life.

forties. Her mother who lived alone in an apple orchard in the Himalayas, was murdered.

Bhabhesh Chandra Sanyal was one of India's foremost sculptors. He had a beautiful and gentle daughter whose pet name was Puchkie. While in college, she fell in love with Kabir Bedi who went on to make a name for himself as an actor in India and abroad. After graduating, Kabir moved from Delhi to Bombay to make a living. He was devastating to look at, tall and light-eyed, and had women swooning over him. Puchkie had to face stiff competition and Kabir broke off with her shortly after coming to Bombay, leaving her heartbroken. Kabir had been a close friend of my sister's while in school in Delhi, and when he came to Bombay, I was one of his very few contacts. One evening, he unburdened himself. He was having an affair with an American diplomat's wife (the American diplomat was having an affair with Asha Putli, the singer!). I introduced Kabir to Gerson da Cunha, then head of Lintas, one of India's leading advertising agencies. Gerson, a stage actor himself, took an immediate liking to Kabir who had also been acting on stage while in college, and gave him a job in his company. Kabir went on to marry Protima Gupta, a sexy and uninhibited model, after they had lived together for some time—a very daring thing to do in those days even in liberated Bombay.

My father got to know Protima quite well. After she separated from Kabir, she became friendly with one of my father's buddies, I.S. Johar, a talented actor-cum-director, but who never really fully used his talents. Johar and Protima even announced that they had got married The news was carried in one of the Bombay newspapers, though whether this was simply a ruse by Protima to get some publicity remains a mystery till date, since both Johar and Protima are dead (she died in a landslide on her way to

Mount Kailash). Protima also got herself romantically linked to Rajni Patel, the well-known leftist lawyer and money-raiser for the Congress Party during Indira Gandhi's days. My father had known Rajni Patel from his student days in England. I don't think he liked the man, and considered him a name-dropping opportunistic phoney. He wrote a scathing obituary on him when he died. My father did not endear himself to Rajni Patel's second wife, the beautiful Bakul. Neither did Bakul ever take to Protima, who made no secret of her affair with Rajni Patel while he was still very much married to Bakul. When Rajni Patel was ailing from cancer and was perhaps somewhat vulnerable, he wrote Protima a series of love-letters, which she was planning to get published after his death. But some powerful friends of Rajni Patel, including actor Dilip Kumar, and editor of *Blitz*, R.K. (Rusi) Karanjia, held her back. Later, she told my father that she had destroyed those letters.

In the late 1990s, my father did a series on TV, called 'Khushwant Singh's Women'. Two of the women he interviewed were Protima Bedi and Persis Khambatta, a former Miss India who also became a moderately successful actress in Hollywood and who too had an affair with Kabir Bedi. Both Protima and Persis died soon after being interviewed by my father. As a result, people used to joke: 'Don't make the mistake of getting interviewed by Khushwant Singh—you will probably die soon after!'

Mangat Rai (Bunchi to his friends), a Christian, was one of the most brilliant Indians of his generation. He studied at Oxford University and then made it to the Indian Civil Service (ICS). He and my father became friends when they were both in their early twenties. Mangat Rai was enamoured of my mother even after he married Champa. My mother admired him and sought his advice on many matters. There was a time when my mother seriously considered leaving my father and marrying Mangat Rai. But perhaps because of the trauma it would cause my sister and me they held back. I only learnt of all this much later. Later Mangat Rai met Nayantara (Tara) Sehgal, Jawaharlal Nehru's niece and Vijaylakshmi Pandit's daughter. They fell in love, though Tara, a very beautiful and talented writer, was considerably older than Mangat Rai. She was trying to get out of a marriage that had gone sour. I am told that after Nayantara's macho Punjabi husband, Gautam, got wind of his wife's feelings for Mangat Rai, he beat him black and blue. Anyway, Tara left her husband, went through a painfully bitter divorce (which became the subject of one her novels) and moved in with Mangat Rai. Eventually they got married and settled down near Dehra Dun. Sadly, Mangat Rai, who had started drinking too much, got Alzheimer's and was bed-ridden. He passed away recently.

Mangat Rai was something of an enigma to me. He became Chief Secretary of both Punjab and Kashmir and was probably one of the outstanding civil servants of his time, admired, even revered, by his colleagues. A man of complete integrity, he steered Punjab through its most glorious period towards prosperity (the dynamic Pratap Singh Kairon was the state's chief minister at the time). Mangat Rai also took over as Chief Secretary of Kashmir at a crucial period and cleaned up the state's administration considerably. But until he met Tara, I think he led a sad, unfulfilled personal life, which probably came in the way of his becoming a bigger public figure than he was. I know that my father, while admiring him as a civil servant, resented the influence he wielded over my mother, though he put up with the situation for a long time. He did not show the pain he must have felt, at least not to my sister and me.

Prem Kirpal, who studied with Mangat Rai at Oxford University, must be the one person whose friendship with my father has lasted the longest. I too regard Prem as a friend, though he is six years older than my father. My father and Prem have known each other for close to seventy years. They were together in Lahore and also in Paris, where both worked for UNESCO. Later, they got together again in Delhi. Prem never married. Though he was engaged several times over, he chickened out each time. Once, he told his fiancée that he had broken his leg. As a doctor she insisted on checking the broken leg. When she found out that nothing of the sort had happened, she took the hint and called off the engagement. My father loved poking fun at Prem, but in a lovable kind of way and Prem took it all sportingly. Though Prem can barely walk now, is losing his memory and has become quite deaf, my father goes over to see him at least once a week, to have a drink with him and keep the friendship going.

Manzur and Asghari Qadir were my father's closest friends in Lahore.

Manzur was a lawyer, like my father. But that was really the only similarity between them. Manzur was very strait-laced, while my father was something of a bohemian. Yet, they got along very well. After Partition, the Qadirs moved into my parents' house in Lahore to prevent vandals from looting or damaging the place. They continued staying there. As I have mentioned earlier, Manzur went on to become Pakistan's foreign minister under Ayub Khan.

I am not sure if I would qualify it as friendship, but my father also got to know Amrita Shergil in his Lahore days. She was an outstanding painter of her generation, and her style continues to influence artists even today. She had a succession of lovers (my father, I should clarify, was not one of them) and led a freewheeling life, as artists often tend to do. When she came to our house, she riled my mother by commenting on how ugly I was! (I was then just a toddler). That was about the last time that she was allowed into our household. Tragically, she died very young.

I mention Amrita Shergil because I recall when I was in my teens, my father took me to a diplomatic function in New Delhi. He had just written a piece on her in his usual uninhibited and candid style, talking about her colourful love life. At that function Amrita Shergil's sister Indira and the sister's husband, a senior civil servant called Sundaram, who became India's Chief Election Commissioner, were also present. He and his wife had clearly taken umbrage to what my father had written. Sundaram was pointedly rude to my father and called him a cheap journalist, or words to that

My father photographed on board R.M.S. Queen Elizabeth.

Raj Villa at Kasauli.

My father has written some of his finest pieces in the peaceful surroundings of Raj Villa named after my maternal grandmother.

effect. Never one to take such abuse lying down, my father lashed back at him, saying just because he was a senior babu, he was not to imagine that he could say and do whatever he liked. Sundaram had probably not been spoken to like that before. There was quite an uproar, with both men shouting at each other before my father walked out of the party, fuming.

The Sundarams had a house in Kasauli where my maternal grandparents also had a home. My father often used to go up to Kasauli in summer. Sundaram's wife spent quite a bit of time there, her husband preferring to live in Delhi. Over the years she became a virtual recluse. Her husband and son, well-known painter Vivan Sundaram, spent little time with her and let her live alone in Kasauli. Her circle of friends began to shrink. Then, one morning, the milkman found that the milk he had delivered the previous morning, had not been collected. The door was forced open and she was found dead. Her husband did not bother to come to Kasauli. When I heard about her sad and lonely death, I recalled with wry amusement how loyally he had come to the defence of Amrita Shergil, probably at his wife's behest, but had left his wife alone to waste away!

Kasauli and Mashobra, a place near Simla, where my paternal grandparents had a house, were great favourites of my father. He loved walking in the hills. Once he even laid bets with his brother-in-law, a strapping fellow called Jaspal, on who could walk faster from Mashobra to Kalka, a distance of over 100 miles. Needless to say, my father won the bet hands down. Later, when I was in college and had started playing a fairly good game of tennis, he laid bets with Jaspal: I could beat his son, Shivi, who was a tall, muscular fellow (I was short and slightly built), and already played for his college. Jaspal had never seen me play and was sure I did not stand a chance against his son. The match took place on the grass courts of the Delhi Gymkhana Club, with both fathers watching with bated breath. To Uncle Jaspal's astonishment and my father's obvious delight, I beat Shivi. I should hasten to add that Shivi was much more successful with girls than I ever was and went on to marry Ruksana Sultan, of the Emergency and Youth Congress notoriety. They had a daughter, Amrita Singh, who became an actress and married Saif Ali, also an actor and the son of 'Tiger' Pataudi and Sharmila Tagore.

My paternal grandfather Sobha Singh's house in Mashobra was a grand affair. Built in the colonial style, it had hundreds of apple, pear and cherry trees, a tennis court, a billiard table and even an underground cellar to store ice (the house was built before long before refrigeration became a commonplace term). My grandfather loved to throw lavish parties and invite all those who mattered in the neighbourhood. This was not entirely because he was a very generous man (he was known for his generosity as well). There was a considerable degree of calculation involved in his entertaining. Every now and then, one of the guests would award my grandfather a lucrative contract. So, the hospitality paid off rich dividends.

I vividly recall being in a pub with some friends in London in 1968 or 1969, near Berkeley Square. An elderly gentleman who had spent some years in India got into a conversation with me. During the chat he mentioned that he had been to Mashobra and had been entertained by Sir Sobha Singh. When I told him that Sir Sobha Singh was none other than my grandfather, he was astounded. I am sure that if the gentleman in the pub had been in a position to award a few lucrative contracts and I had been on the lookout for such contracts, I would certainly have got one that evening!

BBC

A Stint in the Foreign Service

5

It is the mark of an educated mind to be able to entertain a thought without accepting it.

—Aristotle

It was while my father was in Lahore as a lawyer that World War II broke out. Netaji Subhash Chandra Bose had thrown in his lot with the Japanese. Though an admirer of Bose, my father did not agree with him. He was convinced that the fascists had to be defeated first, and favoured the Indian war efforts in support of the British. With the end of the war, the Labour Party came to power in Britain, with Clement Atlee as Prime Minister. Indian Independence was round the corner but marred by the terrible communal bloodshed of Partition. My father witnessed this in Lahore, and while travelling in the countryside in north India, in what would later become Pakistan. Those experiences would form the essence of his first novel, the prize-winning *Train to Pakistan* (which was initially titled *Mano Majra*, the name of the village where the main events in the novel take place). When riots broke out in Lahore, my mother, my sister and I were sent to Kasauli to stay with my maternal grandparents.

Everybody thought the trouble would blow over. It did not. My father also packed his bags and drove from Lahore to Delhi, hoping to return some day. India and Pakistan were born in 1947 after much bloodshed. Partition was one of the saddest chapters of my father's life, as it must have been for many others. And ever since, he has sought to undo it.

FACING PAGE:

With Krishna Menon in 1949 during a broadcast for the BBC in London.

Krishna Menon was then the Indian High Commissioner in London, and my father his Press Officer. Initially, my father was a great favourite of Menon but grew increasingly uncomfortable about Menon's behaviour. My father wrote a devastating exposé on Menon in Opinion.

PREVIOUS PAGE:

With Pandit Jawaharlal Nehru (second from left) at the 1st Commonwealth Prime Ministers' Conference in London.

RIGHT:

With Eamon de Valera, President of the Irish Republic.

President Valera at a formal reception hosted in his honour at the Indian Embassy in London, having a word with Krishna Menon, the Indian High Commissioner in London, my father (extreme right) and my mother (extreme left).

However, Partition and India's Independence had a positive fallout for him. The new Indian government was looking for qualified people willing to join the civil service. After an interview, my father was selected for the diplomatic service, and deputed as the Public Relations Officer (PRO) at the Indian High Commission in London.

The Indian High Commissioner at the time was Krishna Menon. Very close to Nehru, he had promoted the cause of Indian Independence while in London. Menon had a sharp mind and Nehru was in awe of his intellectual prowess.

I think my father liked Menon in the beginning and Menon too grew very fond of my father. But the more he worked with Menon, the more disillusioned he became with him. He found Menon to be mean, corrupt and an inveterate liar who bullied his juniors and fawned over those whom he felt could further his interests. My father could never understand how Nehru did not see through him, or why he is considered an icon in Kerala—the land he hailed from but where he had hardly lived.

With Sarvapalli Radhakrishnan, President of India.

Radhakrishnan was a close friend of my parents before he became the President of India. He was a scholar and wrote several books on Hinduism. On Radhakrishnan's right is M.S. Randhawa, an outstanding ICS officer who played a crucial role in the development of Chandigarh.

One of my father's finest pieces was on Menon. It was published years later in a little-known journal called *Opinion*, edited by A.D. Gorwala, an outstanding member of the ICS, who turned editor and writer after leaving the ICS, and who bravely opposed Indira Gandhi's Emergency.

I think it was partly due to Menon that my father decided to leave the diplomatic service. But while on long leave, before returning to India, he worked on a history of the Sikhs and also wrote the first draft of *Mano Majra*. He also collected some of the short stories he had written earlier in Lahore and England and put them together in a book, entitled *The Mark of Vishnu and Other Stories*, which was published by Saturn Press. A *History of the Sikhs* was accepted by George Allen and Unwin and published as *The Sikhs*. My father also translated Guru Nanak's morning prayer, *Japji*, into English. While the first two books did not do too well in terms of sales, his translation of *Japji*, one of the finest things he has done, does brisk sales even today.

A Literary and Cultural Journey

6

*There are more things in heaven
and earth, Horatio, than are dreamt
of in your philosophy.*

—William Shakespeare

After returning to India in 1950, my father completed his first novel, *Mano Majra* and sent it to Grove Press in the USA. At the time, Grove Press was holding a competition for the best work of fiction from India. Since one of the judges was Krishna Menon, my father decided to use a friend's name instead of the real author's. To his surprise, he won the competition, and a prize of money $1,000, a fairly substantial amount in those days. Along with the prize, came a contract for publishing the book. *Mano Majra* was finally published as *Train to Pakistan* in Britain. At last, he had got recognition as a writer. My father may well have been, like some novelists, a one-novel person.

Without a job, he learnt that the external services of All India Radio (AIR) were looking for producers of programmes. He applied for the English section and got the job. Soon enough he discovered that he had very likeable and interesting colleagues—the writer Nirad C. Chaudhuri and Mehra Masani, the sister of M.R. (Minoo) Masani, one of the founders of the Swatantra Party. Mehra Masani went on to become AIR's first women Deputy Director-General. But to my father's dismay, he found that he had not much work to do, and was spending most of his time gossiping and drinking tea or coffee. Two years into this life he

FACING PAGE:

The family in London.

One of the first few photographs of the entire family taken in London when my father was posted there in the Indian High Commission.

bailed out. Luckily, another job, this time in Paris, beckoned him.

The Director General of UNESCO was in India and on the lookout for somebody for his organization's mass communications department. The person would look after the press, and the radio and films divisions. So in 1954, all of us landed in Paris, my father with a five-year contract with UNESCO in hand. I was fourteen years old and my sister, nine. First I was put into an American school, from where I was taken out after a year because I had not picked up much French. Then I was put into a lycée—the name given to state-funded schools. The lycée I joined was Lycée Lakanal, one of the best in France.

At first we lived near the Eiffel Tower, in the heart of Paris, but later moved into a suburb, Bourg La Reine, in a house that had a small garden with an apple tree. We also acquired a kitten that my father named Simba, Swahili for lion. A cat that belonged to one of my father's colleagues in UNESCO had had a litter. The colleague's family could not keep so many kittens and was planning to drown them—the tragic fate of unwanted kittens at the time. My father decided to take one of the doomed litter under his wings.

Simba grew up to be an unusual cat. Like a dog, he came with us for walks. Once, we went on a long holiday and left him with some friends who lived quite a distance from our house. Just before we returned, Simba somehow found his way back to our place. Sadly, when we finally left France in 1956, once again we had to leave him with some friends. Later we learnt that after staying with these friends for a few days, Simba disappeared never to return.

Our close family friend, Prem Kirpal, was also working at UNESCO at the time and we used to see a lot of him, often spending our weekends and holidays together. My mother

and Prem would often go sightseeing and shopping together (my father hated shopping). Prem loved to recount how my father, during a walk on a weekend, once met a UNESCO colleague of Prem in the neighbourhood where my father lived. 'Do you always come and stay with Mr and Mrs Kirpal during the weekends?' he was asked!

My father had learnt to ski while in Canada, so he would go skiing in Switzerland very often. I picked up the sport quite quickly and became fairly good at it.

A fine balance.

My father was very fond of skiing and Switzerland was his favourite skiing destination.

Apart from Prem Kirpal, another senior colleague of my father in UNESCO was Malcolm Adiseshiah, a somewhat pompous and self-important man. My father did not like him much, and his feelings were fully reciprocated. Malcolm

With the celebrated actress, Ingrid Bergman (extreme right) in Paris.

Bergman was married at the time to the Italian film director, Roberto Rossillini, who was about to come to India to make a film and wanted some advice from my parents. While in India he met and fell in love with Sonali Dasgupta, causing a huge scandal. He would later divorce Bergman and marry Sonali.

Fine friends.

My father (extreme left) makes a point while his one-time colleague and close friend Nirad C. Chaudhuri (second from left) looks on. Also seen in the picture is the Icelandic Nobel-Prize winner, Halldor Laxness, (second from right), another very close associate.

Adiseshiah came into my life much later, in the late 1970s, after he had more or less retired from active life. *Reader's Digest*, of which I was then editor, made him the Chairman of its board of directors. Since I was also a director, we met several times. He was not particularly friendly, on account, I am sure, of his earlier mixed feelings towards my father.

UNESCO was an easy-going place and my father did not have much work to do. He stayed on in the job for two years, mainly because of the lure of living in Paris, arguably the most beautiful and exciting city in the world. He once took me on a driving holiday, along the Loire River, which is dotted with a string of historic chateaux. He had bought a Mercedes Benz with the $1,000 prize money that he had won for *Mano Majra* and it was in that car that we toured the Loire Valley. In the course of this tour we ran into Karan Singh, the former Maharaja of Jammu and Kashmir. He had just got married and was on his honeymoon. His wife, Yasho

Rajya Lakshmi, was strikingly beautiful and they both made a very nice-looking couple.

Another famous couple we met during that trip was the Swedish actress, Ingrid Bergman, and her husband, the famous Italian film director, Roberto Rossellini. Ingrid Bergman was already a big star in Hollywood when Rossellini came into her life. The two fell in love, and she left her American husband to move in with Rossellini in Paris. This shocked the American public and for a long time after that, she did not act in Hollywood films. Rossellini sought out my father because he was preparing to visit India to make a series of documentary films there, and wanted to gather information on the country. We were also invited to his apartment for dinner. He showed us his latest film, *Stromboli*, in a small theatre that he had in his apartment. The film starring Ingrid Bergman had not done particularly well at the box office. Stromboli is the name of a volcanic island in the Mediterranean Sea, off Naples. Ingrid Bergman and Rossellini had a house there. In 1990, I happened to be holidaying on that very island and visited the same house.

Rossellini came to India to make his documentary films and fell madly in love with a beautiful Bengali lady, Sonali Dasgupta (who was already married). The affair became a huge scandal and Rossellini had to leave India. Eventually he left Ingrid Bergman and married Sonali. Rossellini died some years back but Sonali lives in Italy and has a grown up son who is also into filmmaking.

Another of my father's passions was the flamenco, a Spanish dance strongly influenced by the Muslims who had ruled over Spain for many centuries. Flamenco combined ballet with Asian dance traditions, like kathak, but was unique in itself, the music being very Arab. We often went to restaurants in Paris where the flamenco was performed.

The Historian and the Editor

7

What is the good of your stars and trees, your sunrise and the wind, if they do not enter into our daily lives?

—E.M. Forster

In 1956, though my father had three more years to go according to the contract, he decided to quit UNESCO, without another job in hand. Everyone thought he had lost his mind. How else could he leave a cushy tax-free United Nations job? Back in Delhi, he was persuaded to run *Yojana*, a government publication intended to publicize five-year-plans. Though my father tried to liven it up, the paper was a disaster. Nobody was interested in it, knowing that it was government propaganda. But he had some interesting colleagues, two of whom became close friends: Sheila Dhar, an amateur classical singer married to P.N. Dhar, who later became a powerful aide of Indira Gandhi, and T.S. Nagarajan, who made a name for himself as a photo-journalist.

Luckily for my father, just as his interest in *Yojana* was flagging, he met a project scout from the Rockefeller Foundation. The scout had read a short book on the Sikhs that my father had written while in London with the Indian High Commission. The scout suggested he do a more definitive work on the history of the Sikhs and submit a project proposal to the Rockefeller Foundation. To my father's delight, the proposal was approved. The proposed research for the book was to be carried out in Delhi, London

FACING PAGE:

Forever young.

My father's beard starting to grey when he was still in his 20s. When the same thing started happening to me, my grandmother told me that premature greying ran in the family. Many people are amazed that my father's beard is dark and mine completely grey. The mystery? He dyes his beard, I don't.

(India Office Library), Canada and the USA, with a large Sikh population, and also in Japan, Burma and Singapore, since many Sikh soldiers had settled in these countries after joining Netaji Subash Chandra Bose's Indian National Army (INA) during World War II. After failing to get Delhi University to sponsor his work (the then vice chancellor, V.K.R.V. Rao was discourteous and rude to him), he was able to get Aligarh Muslim University to sponsor the project.

I think the four years my father spent writing his two-volume history of the Sikhs were the most rewarding years of his life. They gave him a greater sense of satisfaction than anything he had done earlier as a lawyer, a diplomat or an editor. The icing on the cake came when Princeton University Press, one of the most prestigious publishing houses in the world, agreed to publish the two volumes. From those two volumes came two spin-offs, a biography of Ranjit Singh, the Sikh Emperor, and an account of the Anglo-Sikh wars fought after Ranjit Singh's death.

After the two-volume history of the Sikhs had been published, my father was much in demand abroad as an academic. An amusing turn of events indeed, considering that he had done so badly in his university exams and had no Ph.D. to append to his name. The first invitation came from the University of Rochester, followed by one from Princeton University, where he taught a course on Comparative Religion. At Princeton, he got to know Louis Fischer, the biographer of Mahatma Gandhi and Lenin. After Princeton, he was invited to teach Indian Religions at the University of Hawaii. His final teaching assignment was at Swarthmore College, a Quaker institution close to Philadelphia.

While he was still there a renewed offer (the first offer had been made just when he was about to do his two-volume history of the Sikhs) came from *The Times of India* management to take over as editor of *The Illustrated Weekly of India*, one of the many publications of the *Times* stable. My father was told that C.V. Raman, the then editor, was about to be fired. My father decided to take up the job even though it meant moving to Bombay. At the time I was an assistant editor with *The Times of India*, but readying to move on. The *Reader's Digest* was looking for its first Indian editor and I was picked up for the job. Luckily I had just completed my five-year commitment to *The Times of India*. I was then a little over twenty-eight years old. One of the decisive factors behind my move was the awkwardness of working in the same organization as my father. People were bound to say that I was there because of him. So the *Reader's Digest* offer was not only a very good offer, but a well-timed one as well.

Having accepted *The Times of India* offer, my father needed to find a place to stay in Bombay While working for *The Times of India*, I had lived as a paying guest with Amy and Firdaus Jehangir. My father asked me if he could replace me as a paying guest. I was a little taken aback as were the Jehangirs. But they were only too happy to have him. They spruced up and air-conditioned the room I occupied almost till the very day that my father moved in, and I moved to London for a year's training with the British *Reader's Digest*.

In London, I did something which I now know was very hurtful to my parents: I cut off my long hair (though I kept my beard). You have to be a Sikh, or know the religion and the community well, to appreciate what a drastic step it is for a Sikh to cut off his or her hair (though it is a less drastic step for a Sikh girl to do this). Orthodox Sikhs attach great value to preserving the five Sikh religious symbols, the main one being *kesh*, or hair. My parents were certainly not orthodox (my father liked to call himself an agnostic) but both of them had strong sentiments about the symbols of the Sikh

religion. After all, they had both been brought up on Sikhism, going regularly to the gurdwara or to the room in their parents' house where the *Guru Granth Sahib*, the holy book of the Sikhs, was kept. My upbringing, however, had been different. Neither my sister nor I had been brought up in a religious atmosphere. Yet, somehow—and I thought, unfairly—my parents expected me to feel to share their feelings about the symbols of the Sikh religion. One could be a Sikh, without having to wear a turban or sport a beard (plenty of Sikhs, perhaps most of them, have now discarded these symbols), I felt. What is more, I did not want to look radically different from the others.

When I was abroad, in the '50s and '60s, I would be gawked at, as if I were a being from outer space. That made me feel terribly awkward. In those days, turbaned Sikhs living and travelling outside India were few and far between. On two occasions that I recall vividly, my turban was a cause of acute embarrassment, even pain, for me.

Once, in Paris, when we had gone on an outing and I was too young to have sprouted a beard, I wanted to go to the restroom and naturally entered the one labelled *Hommes* (men, in French). The lady attendant outside the restroom caught me by the collar angrily and pushed me towards the restroom labelled *Femmes* (women, in French). I protested but she was adamant, reducing me to tears and compelling me to call my father. He explained to her that I was indeed a boy and not a girl. She had imagined that my turban was a fancy new headgear for girls!

On another occasion, also in Paris, things were less laughable. One day, while returning from school, I was looking at a window display. Suddenly, I was grabbed and thrown to the ground by a Frenchman who then started kicking me violently. Soon a crowd had collected at the spot and had to restrain him. Shaken to the core and utterly bewildered, I got back on my feet. Somebody then explained to me that the man had been drunk and thought I was an Algerian because of the turban I was wearing, and that he had lost his son in Algeria (the Algerians were then fighting for independence from France).

Once back home, I told my parents about what had happened. My father was shocked and wanted to go back to the place where I had been knocked down, and register a complaint with the police. But eventually we decided that there was little point. I had not been hurt and we could perhaps try and understand the feelings of the man who had struck me, who had lost his son and had mistaken me for an Algerian, a word he had come to hate. But had I been older

FACING PAGE:

In conversation with Zia-ul-Haq in Islamabad, just after he had hanged Zulfikar Ali Bhutto.

My father was then Editor of The Illustrated Weekly *and interviewed Zia who was later assassinated. A bomb planted in his plane exploded, killing all on board, including the US Ambassador to Pakistan.*

At the book launch of *The Sikhs.*

My father addresses a few queries about The Sikhs *during the book launch organized by Roli Books, the publishers of this book, while my sister Mala looks lost in thought.*

and more mature, I would have found it easier to take all this in my stride.

Anyway, I was still in my twenties when I cut my hair in London and tried to justify it by writing to my parents that there was a constant rash at the back of my neck that the doctor said was aggravated by my long hair (which was a fact), but they saw through my excuse. When I returned to India and faced my father without a turban, he was both shocked and hurt and told me to put on my turban. I could not and have not done so ever since. Once the deed was done, there was no going back, though I know of quite a few Sikhs who, despite having cut their hair, put on turbans when necessary. I did not want to be such a hypocrite. Having said this, I must admit that, in hindsight, there are times when I have regretted cutting my hair. I do believe that the turban and the beard impart a certain sense of identity and pride to

the Sikhs, even though some of the very orthodox Sikhs carry this a bit too far.

After the initial awkwardness between us, my father and I settled down to a routine, with me working in Bombay as the editor of the *Reader's Digest* and he as the editor of *The Illustrated Weekly*. My mother came down to Bombay briefly but preferred to return to Delhi. My father lived alone in Bombay but since he was in a very high-profile job, he was a much sought-after person.

Before my father made a foray into Indian journalism, editors had been largely known to maintain a low profile. The only high-profile editor around then was perhaps R.K. (Rusi) Karanjia, the editor of *Blitz*. My father became India's first celebrity editor. He also changed Indian magazine journalism. Under him, *The Illustrated Weekly* carried a mix of titillating pieces and serious articles.

It was a heady combination that succeeded phenomenally. The circulation shot up from around 100,000 copies to 420,000 copies a week. Issues on various Indian communities were huge and unexpected successes, as were the issues on cricket. He also wrote a regular and irreverent column which had a logo done by Mario Miranda, the cartoonist of *The Illustrated Weekly*. The logo showed my father in an electric bulb, a glass of Scotch whisky (his favourite drink) in hand. To this day he uses this logo which has become something of a trademark, in his popular column, 'With Malice Towards One and All.' By and large, he had a young and loyal staff working for him, three of whom

A favourite author.

My father regales all those who had gathered on the occasion to felicitae him and the publisher in his usual inimitable style.

A prolific writer. *My father has written on a wide range of subjects including an authoritative account of* The History of the Sikhs. *Although many of his books have received mixed reviews, he has continued to write, and seems to have become even more prolific with age.*

went on to become successful editors in their own right: M.J. Akbar, Bachi Karkaria and Bikram Vohra. J.I.S. (Jiggs) Kalra turned to cooking and is one of India's most successful chefs and cookbook writers. He still calls my father his guru. Ramesh Chandran became the Washington correspondent of *The Times of India*. At a time when publications were most reluctant to give bylines, even to senior staff, my father allowed his staff to have their own bylines. While this gave them a high, it also made them work very hard. Sadly, two of those mentioned above once misused their positions. In return for carrying a photo that publicized a hotel on the cover, they were given what in journalistic parlance is known as 'freebies'. My father discovered this and sought an explanation. One of the guilty broke down, admitted his guilt and begged for forgiveness. My father took him back. The other, too proud to apologize, was thrown out of *The Illustrated Weekly* (another *Times* publication took him in).

My father's closest friends in those days were Rafiq and Fatima Zakaria. Rafiq was a minister in the Maharashtra government and Fatima was my father's assistant editor. Another very close friend was A.G. (Gafoor) Noorani, a lawyer-cum-journalist. Fatima was in charge of a part of my father's official existence, screening those who wanted to meet him. Gafoor was a walking and eating companion. But he needlessly antagonized the Zakarias and Gafoor by lampooning them in his later writings (including his autobiography). An obviously hurt Gafoor maintained a dignified silence; an enraged Rafiq Zakaria denounced my father in a vitriolic full-page article in *The Asian Age* (edited and published by M.J.Akbar, who still worships my father!). Needless to say, neither the Zakarias, nor Gafoor Noorani are on speaking terms with my father any longer.

Khushwant Singh
RANJIT SINGH
MAHARAJAH OF THE PUNJAB
1780-1839
KHUSHWANT SINGH
A History of the Sikhs
Volume 1 : 1469-1839
KHUSHWANT SINGH
I SHALL NOT HEAR THE NIGHTINGALE
KHUSHWANT SINGH
DELHI
Roman
JAPJEE
SIKH MORNING PRAYER
Translated by Khushwant Singh
INDIRA GANDHI RETURNS
Khushwant Singh
Nature Watch
KHUSHWANT SINGH
SUDDHASATTWA BASU
Khushwant Singh
INDIA
An Introduction
WOMEN & MEN IN MY LIFE
KHUSHWANT SINGH
THE SIKHS
RAGHU RAI
KHUSHWANT SINGH'S
Big BOOK of malice
A Man Called KHUSHWANT SINGH
Edited by ROHINI SINGH
KHUSHWANT SINGH'S JOKE BOOK-II

THE LAST OF THE
BOTCHAN
SORRY, NO ROOM R.K. LAXMAN
No Man's Time
RIDERS IN THE CHARIOT
SIGNAL FIRES OF LACHISH
The undefeated

The Emergency and a Firing

8

I have, indeed, no abhorrence of danger, except in its absolute effect—in terror.

—Edgar Allan Poe

The success of *The Illustrated Weekly* attracted the attention of the powerful, and power in those days lay in the hands of Indira Gandhi and her ambitious son, Sanjay. I am not sure exactly how my father met Sanjay but they hit it off immediately. My father found the programmes Sanjay was trying to implement, especially on family planning, admirable and was in favour of the slum clearance, anti-dowry and grow-more-trees campaigns. He also carried a cover story on Sanjay's 'Maruti: The People's Car' project. It wasn't long before my father began to be associated closely with the Gandhi family.

When Indira Gandhi declared the Emergency in 1975, my father was dismayed. For three weeks, he refused to publish *The Illustrated Weekly*. When he was compelled to resume its publication, he gave instructions to not publish pictures of either Indira Gandhi or her ministers. On the other hand, Sham Lal, the editor of *The Times of India*, even refused to protest the censorship imposed on the press during the Emergency, while Inder Malhotra, the second most important person in the organization, sat on the fence. In any event, given my father's closeness to the Gandhis, no action was taken against him.

The Emergency was not by any means my father's most

Interesting times. *My father debating the Emergency with a guest. At home, we were clearly divided into two camps over the relevance of or need for the Emergency.*

With Sanjay Gandhi (centre) and Mahavir Adhikari of the Times of India group.

Many criticized my father for admiring Sanjay, particularly during the Emergency, but he stuck by him through thick and thin.

glorious moment. He felt he had to stand by Indira Gandhi and Sanjay Gandhi, though I am sure he detested much that went on at the time. At home, my mother, my sister and I opposed the Emergency, while my father supported it in his own way, of course.

The moment of reckoning came when the Emergency was lifted and the Congress Party, along with Indira Gandhi and Sanjay Gandhi, was trounced in the general elections that followed. My father must have realized that his days in *The Illustrated Weekly* were numbered. The magazine had such a large circulation that it had become a major influence on public opinion. Any government in power would have liked to have *The Illustrated Weekly* on its side. And the Jains, who owned *The Times of India* group, were then known to keep to the right side of the government. Sure enough, clear signs were sent to the Jains, probably from the new Prime Minister Morarji Desai's son, Kanti Desai, that my father should be removed. This was done by not renewing my father's contract. Though Ashok Jain publicly denied this later, he told my father that the Desais did not want him to stay on as editor and that, as a result of this pressure, Ashok Jain's hands were tied.

In an interview that my father gave to *Surya*, he said: 'Ashok Jain himself volunteered the statement that the Prime Minister (Morarji Desai) had made adverse comments on my association with *Surya*—which I started with the approval of Bennett Coleman India Ltd.—and my continued support of Mrs Gandhi. He has not retracted that statement. However, when it appeared in the press, the Prime Minister, through his Press Secretary, Sharada Prasad, denied that he had ever spoken about me to Mr Jain. The only conclusion I can draw is one of the two is lying.'

My father went on to say that another reason that Ashok Jain had mentioned for not renewing my father's contract was his age—he was sixty-three. But, as my father pointed out, Sham Lal, the editor of *The Times of India*, was allowed to continue as editor well beyond that age. What's more, *The Illustrated Weekly* had done exceedingly well, raking in huge profits with my father at the helm.

Anyone following this sorry business objectively could surmise that pressure was certainly brought to bear on the Jains from the Prime Minister's office and that the Jains, who had other business interests for which they needed the goodwill of the government, as well as some criminal cases pending against them, succumbed to it and fired my father.

Sadly, no prominent editor extended any support to my father at the time. Perhaps they had been resentful of his success.

Successive public denials notwithstanding, why should a successful editor, who had taken a publication to unprecedented heights, have been removed other than due to outside pressures? Be that as it may, *The Times* management went a step further. Fed on false rumours that my father's farewell editorial was going to attack *The Times* management, they killed the editorial and sent my father a termination notice a week before he was due to retire. The notice was signed by Ram Tarneja, the General Manager of the Times group, who used to fawn over my father and ask him for all kinds of favours. As soon as my father read the notice, without saying a word to anybody except Fatima Zakaria, he picked up his umbrella and walked out of the Times building. His successor, M.V. Kamath, who had been with *The Times of India* for many years, was summoned by Tarneja and installed in my father's editorial chair. Ironically, for a long time, over two years I think, he was designated acting editor until he protested!

When I learnt of all this, I was appalled at the behaviour of the people concerned—Ashok Jain, Ram Tarneja and M.V. Kamath (Kamath could have refused to be party to such shallow treatment of a fellow journalist). At the time, M.J. Akbar was the editor of the already firmly established *Sunday* magazine, with a fairly high circulation (it did not survive very long, though, after Akbar's departure). I told him about what had happened. He published the farewell editorial my father had written for *The Illustrated Weekly* (there was not a word of criticism of *The Times* management in it), along with a column by me, detailing how *The Times* management had humiliated my father.

My father left *The Illustrated Weekly* and Bombay with a heavy heart, not just because of the shabby way in which he had been treated, but mainly because, as he liked to say, he had come to regard *The Illustrated Weekly* as his 'baby'. Soon afterwards he said in an interview that perhaps what the Jains had wanted was a 'faceless editor'. And since he was not one, they found that M.V. Kamath fit the bill. Kamath was stung to the quick by this remark and never forgave my father for it, missing no opportunity to vilify him. One such salvo was a review of my father's autobiography. But what hurt Kamath even more was the fact that his taking over as editor coincided with *The Illustrated Weekly*'s decline.

Kamath was followed by other editors. Amongst the last was Pritish Nandy who gave *The Illustrated Weekly* the kiss of death, killing the magazine as he had killed so many other publications that he had edited.

Agent provocateur.
My father at the recording studios, conducting an interview. His gift for making people say things they did not want to, has always been my father's forte. A programme he did for the Indian television, called 'Not a Nice Man to Know' was a runaway hit for this reason.

Return to Delhi

9

The only tyrant I accept in this world is the still voice within.

—Mahatma Gandhi

After being unceremoniously removed from the post of editor of *The Illustrated Weekly*, my father had an offer to edit the declining Bombay daily, *The Free Press Journal*. Instead he decided to return to Delhi and see what he could find there. *The National Herald*, a Delhi daily that had once been a name to reckon with in the print media but was rapidly losing ground, needed an editor. It was virtually a Congress Party paper and, given my father's proximity to Indira Gandhi, it was but natural that she, through one of her cronies, Yashpal Kapoor, offered the editorship to my father. He accepted, mainly because of his loyalty to her, even refusing to take any salary. But *The National Herald* was a lost cause. Despite the long hours that went into propping it up, the decline of *The National Herald* could not be arrested.

The only notable event that took place during my father's editorship was the publication of the famous—or should I say infamous—obscene pictures of Jagjivan Ram's son, Suresh Kumar and his girlfriend. The pictures were made available to most of the editors in the capital, including my father. He did not use them, but *Surya*, a magazine that had been started by Maneka Gandhi with my father's help, when the Gandhi family was relegated to the wings following the Janata Party victory after the end of the Emergency, carried them prominently. I mention

FACING PAGE:
In a pensive mood.
My father is an early riser and does not lose much time before putting pen to paper for a few hours.

this because, much later, Maneka was able to hold up the publication of my father's autobiography *Truth, love and a little malice* for five long years, on the grounds that what he had written in it on her was an invasion of her privacy, until the High Court allowed the publication of the book, a decision which was upheld by the Supreme Court, which is presently examining the entire issue of freedom of speech versus the right to privacy. That she should have made such a plea seems slightly strange, considering that she did not bat an eyelid before invading the privacy of Suresh Kumar by publishing pictures of him making love to his girlfriend!

My father was close to both Maneka and Sanjay Gandhi, and stood by them, perhaps foolishly, through thick and thin. However, following Sanjay Gandhi's death in a plane crash in 1980, he parted ways first with Indira Gandhi, then with Maneka. In a typically emotional outburst, my father wrote in one of his columns that the logical successor to Sanjay was Maneka, little knowing that by then Indira had begun to detest her daughter-in-law and had started grooming her elder son, Rajiv, as a successor. Meanwhile, my father became the editor of *New Delhi*, an upmarket magazine that had been started by Aveek Sarkar, the head of *The Anand Bazar Patrika* group. Aveek and my father liked each other. However, *New Delhi* was somehow not able to replicate the success of *The Illustrated Weekly*.

Around the same time, my father was elected to the Rajya Sabha. He had no illusions about this being a sort of reward given to him by Indira Gandhi for his unstinting support of her during and after the Emergency. Nevertheless he was very pleased and felt on top of the world. Soon after the Rajya Sabha nomination came an offer from K.K. Birla to edit *The Hindustan Times*, the largest selling daily in Delhi, its sales reflecting more a habit of Delhi's readers than the excellence of its editorial content. This appointment, too, was courtesy Indira Gandhi and Sanjay Gandhi. K.K. Birla was known to have editors who were close to the government in power. My father's predecessor, Hiranmay Karlekar, virtually emerged from anonymity to become editor of *The Hindustan Times* during the Emergency. He was placed there by Siddhartha Shankar Ray, a former chief minister of West Bengal, and a close adviser to Indira Gandhi just before and during the Emergency.

My father signed a three-year contract with K.K. Birla. He worked hard at the job but, frankly, that did not improve the paper much. It had too much dead wood that he could not get rid of. At the end of the three-year tenure, he looked forward to his contract being renewed. Meanwhile, his relations with Indira Gandhi had become increasingly strained because she believed he was on Maneka's side in their ongoing family feud. It follows that K.K. Birla did not renew the contract. Instead he appointed N.C. Menon as

FACING PAGE:

Greeting Giani Zail Singh, on the day he became President of India.

Zail Singh came to call on my father that day. Though my father was critical of Zail Singh's politics and often poked fun at him, they remained close friends.

FACING PAGE:

At ease with everyone.

With the erstwhile Madhya Pradesh Chief Minister, Digvijay Singh (centre) and cartoonist, R.K. Laxman (extreme left) on a writing assignment in Bhopal. My father considers Laxman not only the best cartoonist in India, but one of the best in the world.

editor. Menon had been part of my father's senior editorial staff but the two had not got along well. My father was disappointed to leave *The Hindustan Times*, but his popular column in the paper continued to appear, and does to date.

Ironically, even though Indira Gandhi thought my father was taking Maneka's side, his equation with Maneka and her mother, Amteshwar, was rapidly changing. Following speculations about Maneka's relationship with Akbar ('Dumpy') Ahmed, my father gave one of his typically indiscreet interviews on Maneka, in which he described her, in a rather male chauvinist fashion, as sexless and flat-chested. It marked the end of their association.

I think my father was a little relieved. He had enjoyed the company of Maneka and her mother at a particular time of his life, though he really had little in common with them. Maneka surfaced later in his life, when she tried to stop the publication of his autobiography. By the time, Maneka had become an out-and-out politician. The petition she had filed in the High Court seeking an injunction against the publication of my father's autobiography stated that some parts of the book (which, incidentally, had been published in *India Today* without Maneka taking any action against the magazine) 'violated her right to privacy'.

Though the issue is being mooted by the Supreme Court, I am of the opinion that when a person becomes a public figure, his or her private affairs are of particular interest to the media. The public has a right to know if those it has elected to high office lead exemplary lives. One need only look at the way the media probes the lives of a nation's elected representatives, including presidents and prime ministers.

Hence, it was more than a little amusing to read in *The Indian Express* an interview Maneka gave to Vrinda

Gopinath, in which Maneka extolled the virtues of 'truth' while attacking my father. 'Here's a person,' she said, referring to my father, 'who met Sanjay twice in his life—once in his house in Mumbai, the next time here (in Delhi) when Khushwant came to ask for a Rajya Sabha nomination. He met Indiraji only once and me five or six times, and he claims he knows us very well.'

To set the record straight, my father used to meet Indira Gandhi almost everyday when he was editing *The National Herald*. He also saw a great deal of her before and after the

FACING PAGE:

A cartoonist's delight.

While my father has caricatured people with words, he has often been subjected to a cartoonist's brush himself.

Emergency. It is rather unusual to make somebody a member of the Rajya Sabha after just one meeting! As for Sanjay, there was a time when he would virtually be in and out of my father's place.

In the same interview, Maneka said Sanjay never gave interviews to anybody, and that the family planning programme during the Emergency was 'created by the Health Minister (Dr Karan Singh)' and not by Sanjay.

Well, Sanjay gave at least one interview and that was to my father for *The Illustrated Weekly*! As for Dr Karan Singh's role in the family planning programme during the Emergency, the Shah Commission Report on the excesses committed at the time clearly establishes that the programme was Sanjay's brainchild.

In that telling *Indian Express* interview, Maneka was asked a pertinent question: How did she reconcile herself to being part of a government (the BJP-led coalition) whose members had led a vicious attack against her husband during and after the Emergency? Her answer was, 'I think of myself as someone who thinks of a job as a "welfare professional".' It's time the world woke up to 'welfare professionals' who are extremely economical with the truth.

But to return to my father, using his vantage point in the Rajya Sabha, he dabbled in politics, especially Punjab politics. The Akali Party, the main party of the Sikhs in that state, however, proved too wily for him. Since he had fallen out with Indira Gandhi, he knew that the Congress would not support him for a second term in the Rajya Sabha. The Akalis indicated that he was their man, but at the last moment let him down. Instead, they supported General Jagjit Singh Aurora, one of the main heroes of the Bangladesh War.

4/5/99

Tryst with Politics

10

Better than a thousand hollow words,
is one word that brings peace.

—The Buddha

Disillusioned, my father decided to part ways with Punjab politics, which was just as well. Not really being a political animal, he was never really cut out for politics. Perhaps in another country—Britain, for instance—he would have been more successful. To be successful in Indian politics, you need, to begin with, considerable funds or a benefactor who can provide you those funds (needless to say, the benefactor will expect something in return when you become a Member of Parliament, or better still, a minister). Then, you have to be a seasoned liar who does not easily get caught out. Truth, principles and public interest, which should be the beacons of a self-respecting politician, are alien to all but a handful of Indian politicians, which is why India remains a highly flawed democracy.

Once my father's tryst with politics was over as was his full-time responsibility of running a publication, he could concentrate on what he does best—writing and relating to people. But here I must mention an event which had a deep impact on my father—Operation Bluestar. In 1984 Indira Gandhi ordered troops to enter the Golden Temple at Amritsar, the holiest shrine of the Sikhs. Though my father was opposed to Sant Jarnail Singh Bhindranwale, the Sikh preacher-turned-terrorist, he believed Indira Gandhi could have had him and the other terrorists flushed out of the Golden Temple in a way that was less offensive to the Sikh

FACING PAGE:

Free to write.

His brush with politics behind him, and freed of the responsibility of running a publication, my father concentrated whole-heartedly on writing

sensibility. Operation Bluestar claimed the lives of terrorists and soldiers, and several hundred innocent pilgrims who were also caught in the crossfire. The Akal Takht in the temple complex was shelled out of existence and even the main temple, the Harminder Sahib, was pockmarked with bullets. The Sikh psyche had been deeply wounded.

In protest my father returned the Padma Bhushan that he had been awarded by the President of India a decade ago. There was an air of foreboding in the country. Indira Gandhi had committed a terrible blunder. She would pay for it with her life. Her assassination by two of her Sikh bodyguards unleashed an unprecedented genocide of Sikhs in Delhi and elsewhere. Close to four thousand Sikhs were butchered. My parents had to flee for their lives, and were taken into the home of a Swedish diplomat. Once they returned to their Sujan Singh Park flat, they were given a high degree of security, with a gunman to escort my father whenever he went out for a game of tennis or for dinner. A tent full of security men was pitched in the garden just outside their flat. The security cover was against Sikh terrorists, as my father had continued to write against them. So rather ironically my father became a Sikh who was being protected from other Sikhs!

My father used to joke about his security. That the threat was real was brought home to us one day when Ved Marwah, then police commissioner and a good friend of my father came home to show him something. The police had just caught the men behind the assassination of General A.S. Vaidya, the Chief of the Army Staff at the time of Operation Bluestar. Amongst other things found on the assassins was a detailed map of my parents' flat, showing the entrances and exits to the flat.

'They were planning to kill you,' said Marwah grimly. 'But we caught them before they could carry out their plans.'

My father did not crack any more jokes about security after that, even though in his typically flamboyant fashion, he told his friends that he could think of no better end than being killed by a Sikh terrorist. Fortunately, after a decade of Sikh terrorism that left thousands dead, the terrorist threat receded. First, my father's gunman, then the other security men were withdrawn.

With Indira Gandhi's death and the rift with Maneka, my father's ties with the Gandhi family, which had in any case

FACING PAGE:

The Padma Bhushan.

My father being awarded the Padma Bhushan by President V.V. Giri at Rashtrapati Bhawan. He returned the Padma Bhushan in protest after Operation Bluestar in 1984, when the Golden Temple was stormed, leading to the death of hundreds of soldiers, militants and innocent pilgrims. Though critical of the government's Punjab policy, he was equally vocal in his condemnation of the Sikh militants, for which he received death threats and had to be provided heavy security.

become tenuous, snapped. The only person in the Gandhi household whom he had not known was Rajiv Gandhi. Rajiv arrived at Cambridge University the year that I left, in 1962. But we had a few friends in common and had got to know each other somewhat. Following his mother's assassination, he became the prime minister, and undertook a five-nation tour abroad, which included the USA. I was part of the press party on that tour and we interacted a bit. After that I lost touch with him but was told that he was unhappy with some of the articles that I had written on his administration (I had started by being an admirer, and then turned a critic).

In October 1990, I happened to be staying with my parents in Delhi and was about to turn fifty. My old friend from Cambridge, Camelia Panjabi, then vice president of the Taj Group of hotels, was also in Delhi.

'Why don't you invite Rajiv to your birthday?' She said to me.

I thought about it and told myself, 'Why not? At most, he could turn down the invitation.'

Having sorted that out with myself, I rang up his secretary and left a message. His secretary got back to me, asking me for my address and said, 'Mr Gandhi may drop in for a short while.' I did not mention this conversation to my other guests. His security people turned up just before the party was to begin, looked around the flat, as well as the entrances and exits to the flat. A few of them took up position unobtrusively at vantage points. Rajiv walked in, to the utter astonishment of my guests some of whom knew him. I thought he would stay for just a few minutes and leave before dinner was served. But he seemed to be in no hurry and was clearly enjoying himself, talking easily to everybody and laying on his famous charm. My parents were anxious to serve dinner.

With Rajiv Gandhi on my 50th birthday.

On this occasion my father told Rajiv that his mother and his brother had both graced his house and he was happy that now Rajiv had done so as well. Having said that, my father announced it was past his bedtime and retired.

'Would you like to stay on for dinner?' I asked him.

'Of course,' he replied.

In the course of the evening, my father went up to Rajiv and said, 'All the members of your family have been to my house, except you. I am so glad that you too have come now.' With that he said, 'It's past my bedtime, so goodnight.'

A few months later Rajiv Gandhi was assassinated. Both my father and I felt that having learnt from his mistakes he would have made a better prime minister the second time round. But fate had willed otherwise.

After his brief and ill-starred flirtation with Punjab politics, my father decided to settle down to the routine of doing his two weekly syndicated columns, the occasional

FACING PAGE:

Yet another day.

The newspaper in hand, my father goes out of the house for a breath of fresh air.

book review and, when time permitted, he would work on fiction as well. He has stuck to this routine for the past decade or so. His regular morning doubles games of tennis at the Delhi Gymkhana Club are a thing of the past. With each passing year, he feels unsteady on his feet. But he continues with his constitutionals at Lodhi Gardens, provided people like my sister, my niece or his numerous lady friends accompany him. His frequent air dashes too have, more or less, come to an end. He finds that the steps to get on and off a plane are too steep for him to negotiate comfortably. He remains a voracious reader, making sure that he goes through every book, especially fiction, that is topical, and that has drawn public attention.

He continues to give advice and extend a helping hand often to complete strangers. At least two or three hours a day are spent talking to such people. Sometimes they resurface in his columns. Foreign journalists, radio programmes and TV channels often interview him or seek him out for sound bytes on a topical issue.

But he hates unpunctuality. If anybody comes later than expected, they are roundly ticked off. If they come very late, they are told that he cannot see them. Once, the TV crew of a leading channel showed up about half an hour late. Despite their entreaties, he refused to let them in.

He also likes hosts who invite him to dinner to stick to their timings. On a certain occasion in Bombay, the head of the company I was working for, invited both of us to his home for dinner at eight. My father decided to make an exception to his usual early-dinner rule this particular time. We turned up at our host's house at eight sharp only to find that the host and the hostess were still having a bath. My father waited for ten minutes, then told me that he was leaving, but that I should stay on. When the host and hostess

emerged at 8.30 p.m., I had to tell them that my father, after waiting, had departed. They were mortified, and rightly so.

My father watches quite a bit of television in between reading, writing and meeting people. News, wildlife and nature channels are his favourites. He makes it a point not to miss Barkha Dutt's 'We The People' and Rajdeep Sardesai's 'The Big Fight'. Listening to Sikh kirtans early in the morning and in the earlier hours of the evening (he takes an hour's siesta in the afternoon, straight after a light lunch at noon) on television has become a habit over the last couple of years. I still cannot fathom why he, an agnostic, does this, except that he once said that it did seem to help my mother during her illness. At seven, he opens his well-stocked bar and imbibes a different kind of spirit—two to three pegs of Scotch whisky with soda and ice. Usually, there are others imbibing with him as well, as that one hour from seven to eight in the evening is virtually considered an open house. But as the clock strikes eight, everyone, no matter how important, is shown the door. That is when he orders dinner, while watching television. Nowadays, he rarely goes out for dinner or has guests over for dinner, except the immediate family. By nine he is snoozing in his armchair and by nine-thirty, he makes his way to his bedroom. An early riser, he is usually up and about by five, when he makes his own tea. The only place he likes to go to outside Delhi, is Kasauli, a hill station, 6,000 feet up in the Himalayas, on the way to Simla. There, my maternal grandparents had bought a bungalow soon after Independence, which my mother inherited. With its wonderful climate, clean mountain air and lack of distractions, the bungalow at Kasauli is where my father likes to write undisturbed.

Besides his short stories, my father has till now written four books of fiction, *Train to Pakistan*, *I Shall Not Hear the*

FACING PAGE:

Admiration for Buddha.

My father is seated next to a wooden, gold-leaf Buddha from Burma, kept in our Kasauli house. The Burmese Buddha was sold to my mother by an antique dealer for a ridiculously low price in the 1950s. I was named after Buddha's son

FOLLOWING PAGE:

A typical winter evening.

In our Kasauli house, when it gets cold, a logfire is lit. Above the mantlepiece is a sketch (later made into a painting) by one of India's best-known painters, M.F. Husain, depicting Indira Gandhi as Durga. He did it during the Emergency and was accused of being a sycophant.

PYRAMID
TRADE MARK
(TRADE MARK "FAIRY")

Nightingale, *Delhi* and *The Company of Women*. I must confess I have read only the first two. *Delhi* and *The Company of Women* got such scathing reviews that I decided not to read them, though I knew that *Delhi* was the culmination of several years of research mainly on the history of the city. The reservations of the critics notwithstanding both *Delhi* and *The Company of Women* were best-sellers, which means that the public certainly liked them. *Train to Pakistan* remains to date his finest work of fiction. In his two-volume *A History of the Sikhs*, he is perhaps at his scholarly best.

Apart from that, my father is probably one of the finest communicators of his generation. He has a marvellous ability to communicate with a bewildering array of people, from the most learned and sophisticated, to the most rustic. And they feel equally at ease with him. Though he feels most comfortable communicating in English (he has even gone on record saying that he considers it his mother tongue), he converses easily in Punjabi, Hindu and Urdu. Gregarious that he still is, he insists though, that anybody who wants to see him must first make an appointment on the phone. As a result, his phone does not stop ringing. He does not have a fax or an answering machine, and being computer illiterate, he is not on email either. He does not even know how to type. His stenographer from his *Hindustan Times* days, Laxman Das, comes to the house twice a week to type out his almost illegibly-written columns and do other secretarial work. My mother looked after the matters of the home and hearth. After her death, my sister dons that mantle.

FACING PAGE:

From the Hatter's.

The negro head was part of a whisk given to my father by G. V. Desani, the author of All About H. Hatter, *probably the funniest novel ever written by an Indian, and a classic. Desani did part of the writing in our Kasauli house.*

My Mother

11

To keep a lamp burning
we have to put oil in it.

—Mother Teresa

The strongest personality in our family was undoubtedly my mother, not my father as most people imagined. She liked to maintain a low profile and hated publicity. She preferred to stay out of the limelight even when my father became a well-known public figure, and never allowed any journalist to interview her. Hence she remained something of a mystery to outsiders.

Her name was Kaval. Her mother was a Bhagat and her father a Malik. One of her uncles, Lieutenant General Prem Bhagat, had the distinction of being the only Indian army officer ever to win the Victoria Cross, the highest honour bestowed by the British for valour in action (he won it for clearing land mines in World War II in the North African campaign).

The Maliks considered themselves to be aristocrats amongst the Sikhs. Freshly converted from Hinduism to Sikhism, they tended to be quite devout, and were very particular about maintaining the Sikh symbol of unshorn hair. My mother's father Teja Singh Malik was an engineer by profession and outstanding in his work. He was knighted by the British (as was my father's father). As an astute businessman, he left behind considerable assets—two lucrative petrol pumps some property and a garment business.

My mother's parents were both very religious, her mother even more so. There was a special prayer room in

FACING PAGE:

Globe-trotting together.

My mother accompanied my father when he travelled to Florence, Italy for a UNESCO conference during his stint at the Indian High Commission in London.

their house in Delhi at 4 Bhagwandas Road, and in Raj Villa (named after my mother's mother, whose name was Raj), their summer retreat in Kasauli. *Granthis* or Sikh preachers, would often be hired at considerable expense in Delhi and Kasauli to recite the *Guru Granth Sahib*. Bhai Vir Singh, a much-respected man amongst the Sikhs for his knowledge of the Sikh scriptures, was particularly close to my grandmother and a frequent guest at Raj Villa.

Quite a bit of her parents' devotion, rubbed off on my mother even though she was not intrinsically a religious person. We did not have a prayer room in our flat in Sujan Singh Park, my father being an agnostic and firmly opposed to any kind of religious ritual. But before every important event in my life—my going to Cambridge for higher studies or to Bombay for my first job—my mother would take me to a quiet corner, recite a prayer, and make me repeat the prayer after her.

My mother with her two first cousins, Brigadier Anant Singh (left) and Ujjal Singh (right). *Since their father had died in childhood, the two cousins were brought up by my maternal grandparents who considered them their sons.*

Though neither she nor my father brought me up in a religious manner, given their own upbringing—my mother's more so than my father's—I sensed that they expected me to remain a good Sikh, and keep my Sikh symbols intact.

You have to be a Sikh, or at least know Sikhs closely, to understand and appreciate how intensely many Sikhs feel about not cutting their hair. I know of families who broke off all ties with their children when the children cut their hair. 'My son is dead as far as I am concerned,' was a common refrain used by Sikh fathers once they learnt that their sons had become *monas* (the word used for a Sikh who has cut his hair). I recall that my father once toyed with the idea of sending me to Haileybury, the famous public school in England that had groomed many British civil servants who had served in India. He made inquiries and, I think, even visited the school. The principal of the school told him that I would be more acceptable in the school if I cut my hair and did not wear a turban. Promptly my parents dropped the idea of sending me to Haileybury!

Sir Teja Singh Malik.

When I want to impress my friends, I tell them that both my grandparents were knighted by the British. But the Maliks regarded themselves far more sophisticated than the 'upstart' Sobha Singh family.

Teja Singh Malik had two brothers, I.S. Malik and H.S. Malik. My mother was very fond of I.S. Malik, an immensely lovable man. His great passion was golf and he became probably the best golfer of his generation, winning the national title more than once (his son, Ashok, emulated him and became the youngest national champion, when he was still in his teens). My mother, however, did not quite take to H.S. Malik, who did combat duty with the British Air Force during World War I, was a member of the coveted Indian Civil Service (ICS). He became the Indian High Commissioner to Canada and also India's Ambassador to France.

H.S. Malik was in Canada and in France when my father was posted in those two countries. But my mother remained decidedly cool towards her uncle, even though in Canada, he

En famille.

A rare photograph of the entire family taken in London in 1950 during one of my grandparents' (right) visits. My grandfather was proud of his diplomat son, and rather unhappy when he traded the foreign service for writing.

was her husband's boss, and in France, he could have been very helpful to my parents.

My mother was a person of strong likes and dislikes (my sister Mala, takes after her). There were no gray areas for her. She either liked somebody or did not. There was not an iota of hypocrisy in her, something I am afraid I cannot say for my father or myself. We both tend to take the easy way out, even if it means being somewhat untrue to ourselves. If she did not care for a person, however important that person may have been, she would not hide her dislike. Despite the fact that the person could be useful

A party in London.

My father hosted a party for his parents in London. My grandfather, Sobha Singh is on the extreme left. In the centre is my grandmother, and to her right are my sister and me. To my grandfather's right is Sir George Abel.

to her, she would not put up with him or her. My father and I, on the other hand, are the kind who put up with all kinds. However, if my mother liked somebody, she would go any length to help that person.

She also had great compassion and patience for people she liked, again more than my father or I ever did. Once, I remember, during my college days, one of my close friends (his parents had died) came across two Swiss youngsters in a park. Both were very ill. He brought them to my home. My mother grumbled at first, saying that it was all very well making these grand gestures but it was she who would end

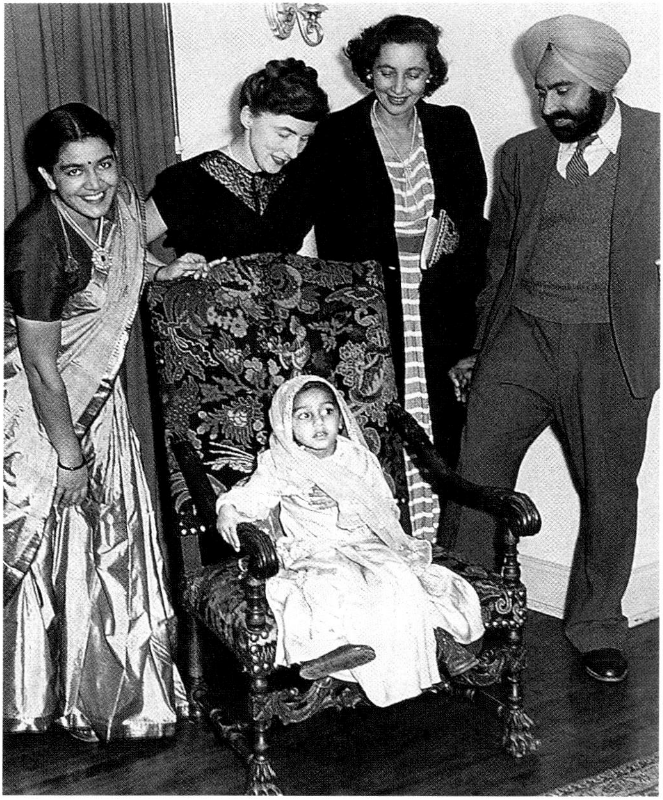

up doing all the work. However, after seeing how sick the two youngsters were and since they really had no one to turn to, she got our doctor to find out what the matter was (acute food poisoning), put them up in our flat and looked after them until they were well again.

With time, I forgot all about them. And then about three or four years ago—that is some 35 years later—the same two Swiss came to India and after making inquiries, turned up at our home in Delhi (I was in Bombay at the time, and my mother was out). They left a touching note behind to simply say that they had never forgotten how my mother had taken them in and nursed them back to health.

'You saved our lives,' they had written. My mother had, of course, forgotten all about it!

On another occasion, when I was studying in Cambridge, my parents came down to England and rented a flat in London during my summer holidays. In college I had made friends with Brian Pollitt (we lived in the same 'digs'). Brian's father, Harry Pollitt, was one of the founders of the British Communist Party and a well-known public figure in the country. Harry Pollitt died during those summer holidays. I went to the funeral and noticed that Brian was very depressed. Though his mother was alive, I sensed that she could not provide the comfort he needed at that particular time. He took to my mother immediately and she also liked him. During that summer, he was at our London flat all the time. My mother had become like a mother to him.

I should add here that my mother was a very good-looking lady. She had the kind of beauty that needed little make up. In fact, she hardly used any make-up, or jewellery for that matter. And she dressed very simply, her favourite being loose *salwar kameezes*. She also had a perfect figure and never seemed to watch her weight. She never went on a diet nor did she work out. She had plenty of admirers, before and after marriage. I remember when she was well into her fifties, a man, who must have been in his thirties used to drop in quite frequently. My mother and he would often to go for walks (my mother was a passionate walker). One day, she came back from a walk and told me how the same person, at least 20 years younger to her, had confessed that he was madly in love with her! I think she was more amused than flattered by his infatuation.

FACING PAGE:

Mala's birthday.

My father was posted as a diplomat in Ottawa, Canada at the time. My mother is on the extreme left and next to my father is Patricia Page, a well-known Canadian poet, who had joined in the celebrations.

FACING PAGE:

Mother and daughter.

My mother and my sister share a light moment in the living room at our Sujan Singh Park house, while Simba, our Alsatian pretends to be clued in.

My father, who could not have been an easy person to live with, and she had an up-and-down relationship. There was a time when my mother's friendship with Mangat Rai evolved to something more intense. My parents were about to split up, but somehow the split never took place, partly I think out of consideration for my sister and me.

Despite their different natures, I believe my father depended more on my mother and her marvellous instincts than he would like to admit. She was closer to my sister than to me, partly because I moved to Bombay when I started working, whereas my sister stayed mostly in Delhi. She disapproved of most of my friends, particularly my lady friends! She had the womanly instinct of seeing through pretense.

My mother kept robust health and rarely fell ill. Everybody else in the family had their aches and pains and their illnesses, but my mother hardly ever. The only time that I can recall when she had to be confined to bed was not really of her own doing. She was taking our pet Alsatian, Simba, for his usual outing to Delhi's Lodhi Gardens. My mother had got in front in the driver's seat and opened the rear door for Simba to get in the back. When she closed that door, she did not realize that Simba's long tail was still not fully inside the car. With my mother's head directly in front of him and the terrible pain of the door slamming on his tail, the poor dog instinctively sank his fangs into my mother's scalp! The gash had to be stitched up and my mother was confined to bed, taking a painful course of anti-rabies injections in the stomach as well. I still recall Simba being so contrite over the incident. He hovered over my mother while she was recovering, with a hangdog look, expressing in near-human ways how sorry he was.

My mother was a great outdoors person, fond of tennis

in her younger years and long walks, until arthritis curtailed her movements somewhat as she stepped into her eighties. Nevertheless, even now a lot of people I meet tell me that the image they have of her is she striding along at a rapid pace in Lodhi Gardens. About six years or so ago, she started falling ill regularly, something that was very uncharacteristic of her. We could not understand why this was happening. She also went into a depression. Perhaps something had depressed her, we thought, and she might need psychiatric help. She, of course, would have none of it. Our family doctor was unable to diagnose what was wrong with her. It was only when we consulted another doctor, a neurosurgeon called Dr Nehru, that he hinted that she could be suffering from Alzheimer's disease—an ailment for which medical science is still trying to find a cure.

A lot of people think that Alzheimer's is nothing but dementia or senility. Not quite so. A person can be afflicted with Alzheimer's at a relatively young age. Its outward symptoms vary. Some people start losing their memory and cannot recognize even their closest friends or relatives. Others become hyperactive and babble a lot of nonsense endlessly. Yet others withdraw into themselves and become totally silent. In my mother's case, it was silence, and withdrawal from the world. But before that happened, some medicines that Dr Nehru gave her seemed to arrest the disease. One fine day, she rang me up in Bombay and announced happily, 'Your Mom has recovered!' But that recovery was only illusory.

Alzheimer's is a terrifying disease that eats into the brain relentlessly. My mother used to, like my father, enjoy her Scotch in the evening—two or three large pegs. She cut down her intake to two pegs that soon dwindled to one till she finally stopped drinking altogether. That was another bad sign.

FACING PAGE:

The apple of my father's eye.

My father holds his only grandchild, his granddaughter, Naina, in his arms, when she was a toddler. Naina is now doing her PhD from Jawharlal Nehru University in Ancient Indian History.

Though no great intellectual, she enjoyed reading a variety of books. She stopped reading, complaining of poor eyesight. I took her to the eye specialist, who gave her new spectacles and said there was nothing wrong with her eyesight. But she refused to read, or even watch television, insisting that she could not see properly. It was pointless arguing with her. She began to spend more and more time in bed and became frailer by the day. Her arthritis made it worse. No more walking for her. She had to be helped even to go from the bedroom to the living room or the bathroom.

Alzheimer's is not only terrible suffering for the person afflicted; it is a huge strain on those looking after such a person. My father, unable to take the pressure of being woken up repeatedly during the night by my restless mother, moved into another bedroom. My sister slept in the bed alongside my mother and we kept a day nurse. We made a pact that I would come down from Bombay to share the responsibility of looking after my mother, with my sister. So, each time I was in Delhi, I would sleep in the bed alongside my mother. My sister and I sensed that my mother felt more comfortable when either of us was with her during the night. But it was fitful sleep at best and we would be exhausted the next morning. My sister came close to having a nervous breakdown and the two of us were constantly snapping at each other. It was one of the most trying times of our lives. Though we would tell her not to get up and go to the bathroom without our help, my mother would get up on her own and start making her way to wherever she wanted to go, often when either my sister or I was asleep. On one such occasion, she fell heavily, cutting herself over the eye and bleeding profusely. Yet, oddly, she seemed to sense no pain.

We decided to keep two nurses, one for the day and the other for the night, to keep a watch on my mother and to help her go to the bathroom. This must have gone on for about two years. During this period my mother spoke very few words, though she seemed to recognize most of the people who came to visit. A number of pills were given to her four times a day. Unable to chew, she was given food either in liquid or pureed form. She progressively became weaker and trying to get her to talk became increasingly difficult. But she liked to sit in the living room, even when my father had visitors. His once hectic social life now almost came to a grinding halt.

Then, one day she woke up, not being able to breathe properly. We summoned the doctor who said she was to be taken immediately to a nearby hospital. Our domestic help picked her up easily in his arms—she was barely more than just skin and bones—and I drove her to the hospital. My father had a pained look on his face as the car pulled away. I think he felt she would never come back home. The doctors there gave her an injection to clear her lungs and she was put on a drip and oxygen. I decided to stay the first two nights in the hospital, sleeping on the sofa in the room, with my sister always there to take over from me. The next morning something quite miraculous happened. My mother was smiling and bright-faced. When the doctors removed the oxygen mask, she started talking—and just would not stop! And it was not nonsensical babble, but normal conversation. She called me by my pet name, something that she had not done for several years, asked me about my various girlfriends. Her mind had suddenly become absolutely clear, as if nothing had happened in the last six years or so. I was a bit incredulous at this remarkable improvement myself. I even had to tell her to stop talking so much because she was exhausting me with her questions!

On one of their holidays together.

My parents in Kashmir at the Dal Lake.

The morning after that I returned home to tell the family of my mother's seemingly miraculous recovery. They too were incredulous. My sister went to the hospital that morning and saw what I had seen the previous day: an apparently cured mother, chatting away, her memory absolutely clear. She, too, found this difficult to believe. Then, the next day, the dream was over. My mother regressed to what she had been earlier, silent, withdrawn and unsmiling. My sister came back to give us the bad news. I pleaded with the doctors. 'She was fine for two days. Why can't you bring her back to that normal state again?' They shrugged their shoulders and said they were helpless. How had she recovered so suddenly for those two days? I asked them. They had no answer and told me that Alzheimer's was so peculiar that there were more questions on the disease than answers to them.

We brought her back home. The doctors told me that there was no point in my staying on in Delhi, so I left for Bombay. A few days later, my sister rang me up in the morning. 'Mom has passed away peacefully,' she said tonelessly.

What we had been expecting for quite a long time had finally happened, though that did not lessen the sense of loss. My father decided that he would not wait on any ceremony and that she was to be cremated that very day, in the afternoon at the nearby Lodhi crematorium. No prayer meetings were held, in accordance with what she had told my father. I was able to get a flight to Delhi only that evening, after the cremation was over.

The next morning my sister, our doctor and I went to the crematorium. My mother's ashes were still smouldering. We said a little prayer, collected the ashes, immersed most of them in the nearby Jamuna river, but kept some to immerse near a gurdwara also located on the banks of the Jamuna. When we got to the place, we found the river there was like a sewer, heavily polluted and smelling foul. There was no question of immersing her ashes here, we decided. They would be used to plant some saplings in Raj Villa in Kasauli, the house that she had inherited from her parents and which she loved so much. Soon after, over a weekend, my sister, her husband, their daughter, my long-time girlfriend, Niloufer and I drove to Kasauli, picked up some saplings from a nursery on the way and planted them in various parts of the garden, along with the remaining ashes. I think she would have approved.

400 East 52nd St. New York, NY 10022
Ruth Jhabvala

December 29

Dear Khushwant,

Renana phoned us today to tell us the sad news about Kawal. Ever since, our thoughts have been full of her, and how some of our happiest moments in Delhi were the evenings we spent as her and your guests. She was such a wonderful, such an easy and natural hostess. I've always admired her beauty — and she was so very beautiful, no wonder everyone was in love with her! I remember her striding in Lodhi Gardens and in Kasauli, in earlier years with her dog — the same dog that accidentally bit her and then was so contrite that we were never allowed to mention the incident in his presence. And I remember her forthrightness – the way she could even get Nirad to stop talking and go home at a reasonable hour.

There are so few of us left now, but how fortunate that all our memories of one another are without a shadow on them – all of them good and beautiful and of great happiness.

Dear Khushwant, Jhab and I send you all our love and all our thoughts to you and Rahul and Mala and Ravi and Naina –

Yours as ever

Ruth

Khuswant Singh—*IL Santo Grande*

12

It is the vice of a vulgar mind
to be thrilled by bigness...

—E.M. Forster

Though my father has given up playing an active role in politics and retired from full-time work in the last decade or so, he continues to be dogged by controversy. He remembers a seminar that was held in Shillong attended by only about a dozen people. In the course of the seminar, he said that he thought Rabindranath Tagore, who won India's first Nobel Prize for Literature, was a vastly overrated writer and, though he was a marvellous writer of songs, his stories and novels were not much good. In fact, my father added that other Bengali writers, who had left their mark on Bengali Literature after Tagore, were better. Clearly my father had hit a raw nerve. The Bengalis have some holy cows—and Tagore is one of them (the others are film-maker Satyajit Ray and freedom-fighter Netaji Subhash Chandra Bose). My father's comments were picked up by *The Anand Bazar Patrika* and when he landed in Calcutta, people were demonstrating outside his hotel to register their protest against what he had said. The West Bengal Assembly and the Rajya Sabha even passed resolutions against my father! The demonstrators said that he should not have criticized somebody they worshipped.

His rhetorical reply to that was, 'Instead of worshipping him, why don't you read him?'

Talking of worship and idolatry, my father strongly dislikes the Indian habit of spending so much time on

FACING PAGE:

Feeding the cats, outside his Sujan Singh Park house.

For some unknown reason, stray cats are attracted to my father and a bevy of them are constantly mewing outside his door for food and affection, both of which they receive in ample measure.

religious rituals. He says, 'Work is worship, but worship is not work. If you sit back and think of the many religious rituals that we have in the country, you would find them quite meaningless,' he once told well-known writer and diplomat Pavan K. Varma. 'I have not spared even my own community,' he related. 'Take the Sikh ritual of *Akhand Path*, non-stop prayer for two days and two nights. What does it mean? The people involved in it are fast asleep at night. The *Guru Granth Sahib* lies in the corner. People go on mumbling something. Even if you are sitting there, it wouldn't do any good. But this kind of ritual is devoid of any reason, and when I write about it, it upsets the Sikhs. They say they don't believe in idol worship. But they treat the *Guru Granth Sahib* as an idol, waking it up in the morning, draping it in beautiful clothes, taking it out in a procession, rubbing their noses in front of it. They don't read it carefully, but they treat it as silk of an expensive kind. In summer they keep air conditioners running in the room where the *Guru Granth Sahib* is kept; in winter they keep it nicely warm in a Pashmina shawl. At the back of their minds the *Guru Granth Sahib* is a human being.'

Another of his close friends, writer and member of the National Commission for Women, Syeda Saiyidain Hameed, sums up his attitude towards religion well: 'I regard him as close to Islam as to Hinduism, to Sikhism and to Christianity. He treats all religions with the same reverence and irreverence. He owns at least six different translations of the Quran. He has done the most fascinating work with the Sikh scriptures. He cannot stand a fanatic nor can he stand a person without humour. Of prudes he is most intolerant.'

Speaking of prudishness, one of the more amusing incidents in my father's eventful life took place at the release of the novel, *The Company of Women*. Amongst those who attended the launch were the Pakistani High Commissioner, Ashraf Jehangir Qazi, accompanied by his wife and two daughters, both in their twenties. My father planted an innocent peck on the cheek of one of the daughters, a common custom in the West and in certain circles even in India. A photographer happened to press the shutter at the right moment and the photograph was splashed in the Indian press. Some elements of the Pakistani media immediately reproduced the photograph and whipped up a frenzy. Certain fundamentalists in Pakistan went to town over the incident and the poor Pakistani High Commissioner was asked to submit an explanation about the incident to the Pakistani government. For once, my father was at a loss for words!

My father got embroiled in another controversy, the one relating to one of the most talked about books of our times: Salman Rushdie's *The Satanic Verses*. Since my father was a consulting editor for Penguin India, the manuscript of the book was sent to him for his opinion several months before it was actually published in India. After reading the manuscript, he felt it could create trouble. To have a brothel in Mecca with some of the girls in it named after the wives of the Prophet was incendiary stuff for orthodox Muslims—and there were quite a few of them around, led by Iran's Ayatollah Khomeini. Though absolutely against censorship, my father recommended that Penguin India have nothing to do with the book. Penguin India, however, went ahead with the publication. The death fatwa on Rushdie and the huge uproar that followed in its wake, however, did bear out his gut feeling about bringing out the book in India.

I am sure that if she could, Kamala Das, the poetess from Kerala, would also have loved to issue a fatwa against my father. My father found out that Das had been floating a

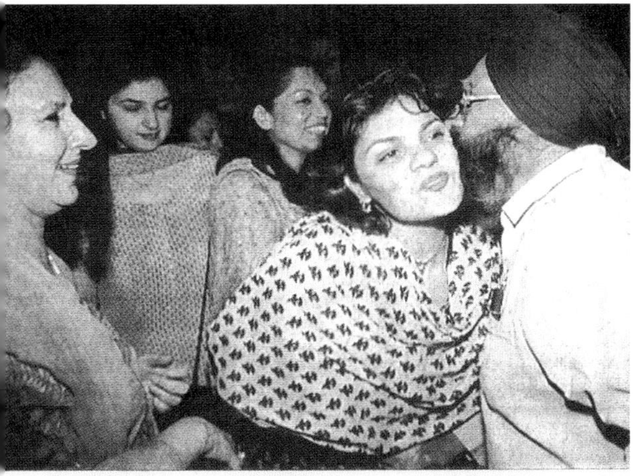

Khushwant Singh with the wife and daughters of Ashraf Jehangir Qazi, the Pakistan High Commissioner, at the launch of his novel *In Company of Women* in New Delhi on Thursday — *Express photo by Mustafa Quraishi*

An innocent peck. Ashraf Jehangir Qazi, the then Pakistani High Commissioner was asked to submit an explanation about this 'transgression' to the Pakistani government.

rumour that she had been nominated for the Nobel Prize for Literature. (Some other prominent Indians had also floated such delusional rumours about themselves). With his typical brand of humour, laced with a little malice, he wrote a column on this. Das was mortified and accused him of being prejudiced against South Indians, a preposterous accusation—and probably the first of its kind—that nobody took seriously.

Her final condemnation of my father was, 'I don't want to meet him in this world.'

Incidentally, one of her sons, Monu Nalapat, a close friend of mine, subsequently slapped a defamation suit on my father for what he had written about his mother.

On a somewhat more amusing note, in the summer of 1970, my father got a fellowship for a month to simply do what he wanted (the fellowship was meant for writers) in a very beautiful locality in northern Italy, overlooking Lake

Como. A fiend for exercise, he found that though the estate where he had been put up, had every amenity imaginable, it did not have a tennis court where my father could exercise. But since he also likes to swim, and there was a lake almost at his doorstep, he decided that he would catch up on his exercise by swimming across the lake to the other side, climbing the hillside there, then swimming right back.

Many may have done that without causing a ripple. But a hirsute Sikh with a flowing beard, long hair, wearing just a *kachcha*? At least the peasants from the other shore, simple folk who cultivated their fields and reared their sheep, had never seen such a sight before in their lives.

Ramachandra Guha, writing in *The Hindu*, had this to say of this incident: 'Nothing in their culture or folklore had prepared them for the sight of a Sardar after his swim. The lord who once lived in the manor house had been seen, if at all, only atop a horse. Of the Americans who later patronized the place, the odd fellow might have entered the water, sometimes, but then he was coloured white, had close-cropped hair and was clean-shaven besides. A week passed, and still the Sardar came, every morning. Another week and the peasants had convinced themselves that this was a saint, *il santo*. By the end of his stay he had been elevated further still, to the rank of 'great saint', or *il santo grande*. So epochal was Khushwant Singh's holiday in the Como Hills that to this day local history is marked by a reference to it. "Do you remember the murder of that inn-keeper," an old man will say, "It happened the winter following the visit of *il santo grande*." '

The Great Saint Khushwant Singh of Lake Como—surely my father must have been amused by that!

One of the persons my father admired immensely was

FACING PAGE AND BELOW:

A Tribute to Mother Teresa.

My father had the article he wrote on Mother Teresa after visiting her in Calcutta, framed along with her photo. Below, in her handwriting is, 'Dear Mr K. Singh, God bless you.'

the Nobel Prize-winning Albanian nun, Mother Teresa, who has recently been beatified. A photograph of her with him still occupies the pride of place in his study at our Kasauli home. E. Le Joly, author of *We do it for Jesus: Mother Teresa and her Missionaries of Charity*, wrote: 'In 1975, *The Illustrated Weekly of India*, the weekly magazine most read by the middle and upper classes in India, displayed Mother Teresa's picture on the cover. In the main story, the editor Khushwant Singh, praised the work of the Missionaries of Charity. Some months later, in August, Mother Teresa told me, "Mr Khushwant Singh's article has changed the

people's attitude towards us. I notice the difference: there are no more misgivings or frowns when we are mentioned. All show sympathy and appreciation for our work. This is really marvellous." ' Joly went on to say that Mother Teresa added, 'Khushwant Singh wrote to me. He wishes to make me meet other newspaper editors when I go to Bombay so that I may talk to them of the poor and their responsibilities to the weaker members of society. He ends with the words, "God bless you." ' It seems Mother Teresa added with a chuckle, '...though I think he is not a believer.'

Mother Teresa was close to the truth. He admires the likes of Mother Teresa, spiritually minded people whose mission in life is to better the lot of their fellow human beings, especially the poor and the deprived. But he detests religion that is sterile, self-centred and full of rituals. He is intrigued by our so-called 'godmen' like the late Rajneesh, whom he admired for his learning. For the most part though, he finds godmen to be bogus, making fools—and money—out of the gullible.

Mother Teresa's success owes much to her remarkable ability to obtain collaboration from every side. She enlisted the help of the Pope, of prime ministers, chief ministers, presidents of various states, and a considerable number of laymen.

She also used all the modern means of mass communication. The media made her known and thus rendered her work possible. They made her first a state, then a national, and finally a world figure. Without the help of the press, the radio and television, her activities would have developed only slowly and would probably have remained confined to India.

'The Statesman,' a leading Calcutta daily, was the first to throw a spotlight on her by mentioning her in its columns. 'The Amrita Bazar Patrika,' another leading daily, followed suit.

English and American ladies spread her fame abroad: *Time* mentioned her several times and carried her photo.

In 1975, *The Illustrated Weekly*, the weekly magazine most widely read by the middle and upper classes in India, displayed Mother Teresa's picture on the cover. In the main story the editor, Kushwant Singh, praised the work of the Missionaries of Charity.

Some months later, in August, Mother told me: 'Mr Kushwant Singh's article has changed the people's attitude towards us. I notice the difference: there are no more misgivings or frowns when we are mentioned. All show sympathy and appreciation for our work. This is really marvellous.'

Mother added: 'Kushwant Singh wrote to me – he wishes to make me meet other newspaper editors when I go to Bombay so that I may talk to them of the poor and of their responsibilities to the weaker members of society. He ends with the words 'God bless you,' she added with a chuckle, 'though I think he is not a believer.'

Dear Mr. K. Singh
God Bless you
M Teresa mc

V. A S NAVELC
Goa - 2001

Through the Eyes of Others

13

This above all—to thine own self be true...

—William Shakespeare

Just before I embarked on this book, I wrote a letter to some publications, requesting readers who might have interacted with my father, or corresponded with him, to send me copies of the correspondence and share their experiences with me. The response was overwhelming and I thought I would share with the reader some experiences which shed light on the kind of person my father is.

S.P. Singh, a retired civil servant from Patna, wrote about how the mountains had claimed the life of his son after the latter had successfully climbed a hitherto unconquered Himalayan peak. 'The Indian Mountaineering Foundation, which had sponsored the expedition that turned out to be fatal for my son, took little notice of the mishap and failed to publicize my son's glory,' wrote the grief-stricken father. 'I brought this fact to your father's notice . . . soon after he wrote an eulogistic piece in his column, with my son's photograph, about his valour and the right of brave people to be remembered. Needless to say that piece gave to my family and me a great amount of solace. That also earned for us overwhelming sympathy from a large circle of mountaineers.'

If my father feels that sufficient recognition has not been given to somebody deserving, he champions that person's cause. As a result, he is besieged by people who

FACING PAGE: From one caricaturist to another.

FACING PAGE:

A love for pets.

My father has always had a special fondness for cats and dogs.

want to see him, and receives countless phone calls not just from India but all over the world. S.P. Singh has never met my father, yet my father could tell by the tone of S.P. Singh's letter that this was a genuine case that deserved greater recognition. Of course those who want to use my father often take him for a ride. Fortunately, the genuine ones far outnumber the manipulators.

In his letter to me as well S.P. Singh made an interesting observation possibly shared by a lot of people. After criticizing my father for not giving the Hindi language its due (S.P. Singh is a well-known writer in Hindi), he adds: 'He is somewhat hypocritical, just as perhaps every Indian is. He takes pride in proclaiming himself an atheist [actually, agnostic is what my father would call himself], still he wears a turban and a beard enjoined as an appearance for those who believed in God.' S.P. Singh then goes on to compare my father to the staunch communists in West Bengal who are as staunch as other Bengalis in their unbridled worship of Ma Durga. S.P. Singh may most certainly have a point, and I think my father would have a tough time explaining his stand.

When Chandra Vijay Singh was a member of the Rajya Sabha, he had an entirely different experience. He met my father at a common friend's house when my father was visiting Moradabad, Vijay Singh's hometown. My father promised to look him up the next time he was in Moradabad, a promise that he kept. Evidently my father was quite taken up by Vijay Singh's wife Harsh. After saying in his column that she was the most beautiful woman he had seen in many years, he described her as, 'tall, slender, ivory-complexioned, lotus-eyed, long-necked and with a full shapely figure'. In his letter to me, Vijay Singh wrote that his wife obviously took my father's column very seriously indeed, 'realizing perhaps

that she was wasting away in the backwaters of Uttar Pradesh. She took off in December that year (the column had appeared in September), never to return!' Wrote a maudlin Vijay Singh! That's the kind of havoc my father's column could wreak in some people's lives! But Vijay Singh's story had a happy ending. 'The replacement I found for my wife is not as tall, but equally endowed in most ways,' continues Vijay Singh in his letter to me. 'And I consider myself lucky. But this time I am not going to let your father make her aware of it—can't afford alimony a second time over!'

FACING PAGE:

Morning walks.

My father is greeted during his morning walk in Kasauli bazaar by a very young well-wisher.

How I wish more Indians had a sense of humour as Chandra Vijay Singh did, and were capable of taking things in their stride with a smile.

Meenakshi Devi Bhavanani's letter to me poignantly brings out another cause my father upholds—the fight for justice. 'He has titled his newspaper column, "With Malice Towards one and All", she wrote to me. 'But I have found no malice in this man in my encounters with him. On the contrary, I have found him deeply humane capable of caring and, more importantly, backing up that caring attitude with actions.' She then goes on to relate how she was born in the USA, but soon after she came to India she fell passionately in love with the country and identified with it and its culture. She went on to marry an Anglo-Indian medical doctor who was a Canadian national, and became an expert in yoga and bharatanatyam. The two of them invested their hard-earned money on a five-acre site in Pondicherry, which they developed and made into a yoga-cum-cultural centre, where poor children also received education and free food and medical aid. As often happens in India, greedy politicians began eyeing their centre since the price of real estate had meanwhile shot through the roof. To cut a long and sordid story short, Meenakshi Devi and her husband were thrown out of their land after being accused of being 'foreigners'.

Desperate and threatened with deportation, they reached out to the national press. My father was amongst the journalists who responded and wrote about their plight and the machinations of the Pondicherry government in his column. Following a national and international outcry, the Pondicherry authorities stepped back. The couple eventually won their case in the Madras High Court and soon after, got their Indian citizenships. 'We would not be here were it not for people like your father with his compassionate and

FACING PAGE:

A ladies' man.

With Baljit Virk, a teacher at the Pinewood School in Kasauli, on the lower mall in Kasauli.

cosmopolitan heart,' wrote Meenakshi Devi to me. 'I say "cosmopolitan" in the real sense of the word, as "someone who is a resident of the cosmos", someone who knows he lives in a universal sphere, not a local frog pond. His kindness, compassion, understanding, intellect, sympathetic words meant so much to us at the time of our trouble, I cannot express myself. I can only forever remember him with admiration and gratitude. Behind that propagandist facade, he is the kindest, softest and most faithful and true of all human beings.'

Kumar Narayan Sarangdhar from Goregaon, Bombay, has written to me saying that though he has never met my father, whenever he gets 'emotionally or mentally disturbed', he seeks and finds solace in my father's books, and that through my father's writings 'à la Dronacharya' he has been inspired to write good English and that he still considers himself to be my father's pupil 'Eklavya'. Sarangdhar adds, 'What is remarkable about him is his easy accessibility to the common people.'

I am often asked, 'What is it like being the son of Khushwant Singh?' Quite a mixed fare, I should say. There have been occasions when I have been asked to preside over a function and the person introducing me has made it a point to mention that I am 'the son of the illustrious writer, Khushwant Singh,' then made haste to add, 'but he is well known in his own right.' I confess I find myself cringing on such occasions. But I do not really mind being displayed at social gatherings as 'Khushwant Singh's son'. Though I might not show it, I am proud of my father.

At times being his son has its distinct advantages. Once I was in the Kashmir Valley, interacting with some of the militants. They were rather wary of me at first but on learning who my father was, the veil of suspicion lifted

immediately and they warmed up to me—an indication of how widely he is known, read and liked.

Despite some of his controversial views, almost everybody I have met admires his honesty, his great sense of humour and his sincerity. 'He often writes nonsense but he genuinely believes it,' is a common reaction even from his detractors. On a couple of occasions when I have been to Pakistan—or met Pakistanis outside Pakistan—I have been treated like a celebrity, solely because my father is liked and admired there for firmly believing that there should be closer ties between the two countries.

Being Khushwant Singh's son, however, has its flip side as well. I was in Washington in 1976, at the height of Indira Gandhi's notorious Emergency. Ashok Mahadevan, then deputy editor of the *Reader's Digest*, had been invited to a party thrown by an Indian who lived in the USA. I tagged along with Ashok. When we arrived at the party, he made no mention either to the host or the other guests, most of who were Indians but who did not know who I was, of my parentage. Inevitably, the conversation veered to the political situation in India and virtually everybody condemned the Emergency, with the choicest expletives being showered on Sanjay Gandhi. And just as inevitably, my father's name cropped up since he was one of the few intellectuals who had supported Indira Gandhi. In hindsight, I should have, at that point, come out clean and mentioned that it was my father they were talking about—and made light of the matter. But I didn't and one of the guests then proceeded to say, 'I wish somebody would shoot that bastard Khushwant Singh.' My friend, Ashok Mahadevan, who had brought me to the party in the first place, looked at me apologetically. His embarrassment was evident. 'Actually, Rahul here is the son of Khushwant Singh,' he announced to the gathering. There

FACING PAGE:

To thine own self be true.

My father experimenting with truth.

was a stunned silence. The host mumbled some apologies. I smiled, somewhat foolishly I think, and said, 'It really does not matter,' or words to that effect. But the party was a complete disaster. The earlier animated discussion petered out, replaced by polite natter.

Though good at heart, my father does like to shock Indian society. Let me quote a critical appreciation of him written in the *Indian Express* by Mushirul Hasan, an academic. After saying that he was neither a friend nor a follower of my father, he wrote: 'But, all said and done, he has kept intact his image of an iconoclast and a non-conformist. That is because he questions conventional wisdom incessantly, challenges political and religious orthodoxies fearlessly (for which he got into trouble with the high priests in the Akali leadership), and flouts established norms and time-honoured conventions, relentlessly. Yet, he is not self-righteous as the late Nirad C. Chaudhuri was. Besides, he is tolerant, eclectic, and intellectually committed to pluralism and multi-culturism. He is the quintessential liberal, one of the dwindling tribe in India of today and I find his outlook much closer to Jawaharlal Nehru's worldview than that of any other public figure in the 20th century.'

Mushirul Hasan also praises him for promoting Urdu: 'He is amongst the very few who, unmoved by the linguistic claptrap, has introduced the richness and bewildering variety of Urdu to English-speaking readers.' He concludes that, 'Some people may have complaints about Khushwant Singh, yet they would find it difficult to deny that this man has done so much to enrich our cultural and intellectual life for well over three decades. As an outsider to the capital of India, it is hard for me to think of Delhi without him.'

My father often likes to quote a poem by James Henry Leigh Hunt entitled *Abou Ben Adhem and the Angel*. It touches a sensitive chord in the humanist in him:

Abou Ben Adhem (may his tribe increase!)
Awoke one night from a deep dream of peace,
And saw—within the moonlight in his room,
Making it rich, and like a lily in bloom—
An angel writing in a book of gold.
Exceeding peace had made Ben Adhem bold,
And to the presence in the room he said,
'What writest thou?'—The vision raised its head,
And, with a look made of all sweet accord,
Answered, 'The names of those who love the Lord.'
'And is mine one?' said Abou, 'Nay, not so,'
Replied the angel. Abou spoke more low,
But cheerily still; and said, 'I pray thee then,
Write me as one that loves his fellow men.'
The angel wrote and vanished. The next night,
It came again with a great awakening light,
And showed the names whom love of God had blessed,
And lo! Ben Adhem's name led all the rest.

Despite my father's ability to befriend people from all walks of life, he has made many enemies. But he takes their onslaughts in his stride with his inimitable humour. He loves to show visitors a letter sent to him from Canada by a Canadian Sikh. It is not the contents of the letter, however, that he enjoys showing but the envelope in which it arrived. It was addressed to: 'Khushwant Singh, Bastard, India.' The letter was delivered to him! Well, the 'Bastard' is now pushing ninety and continues to infuriate his foes and delight his admirers alike.

Mulling over his
next book.

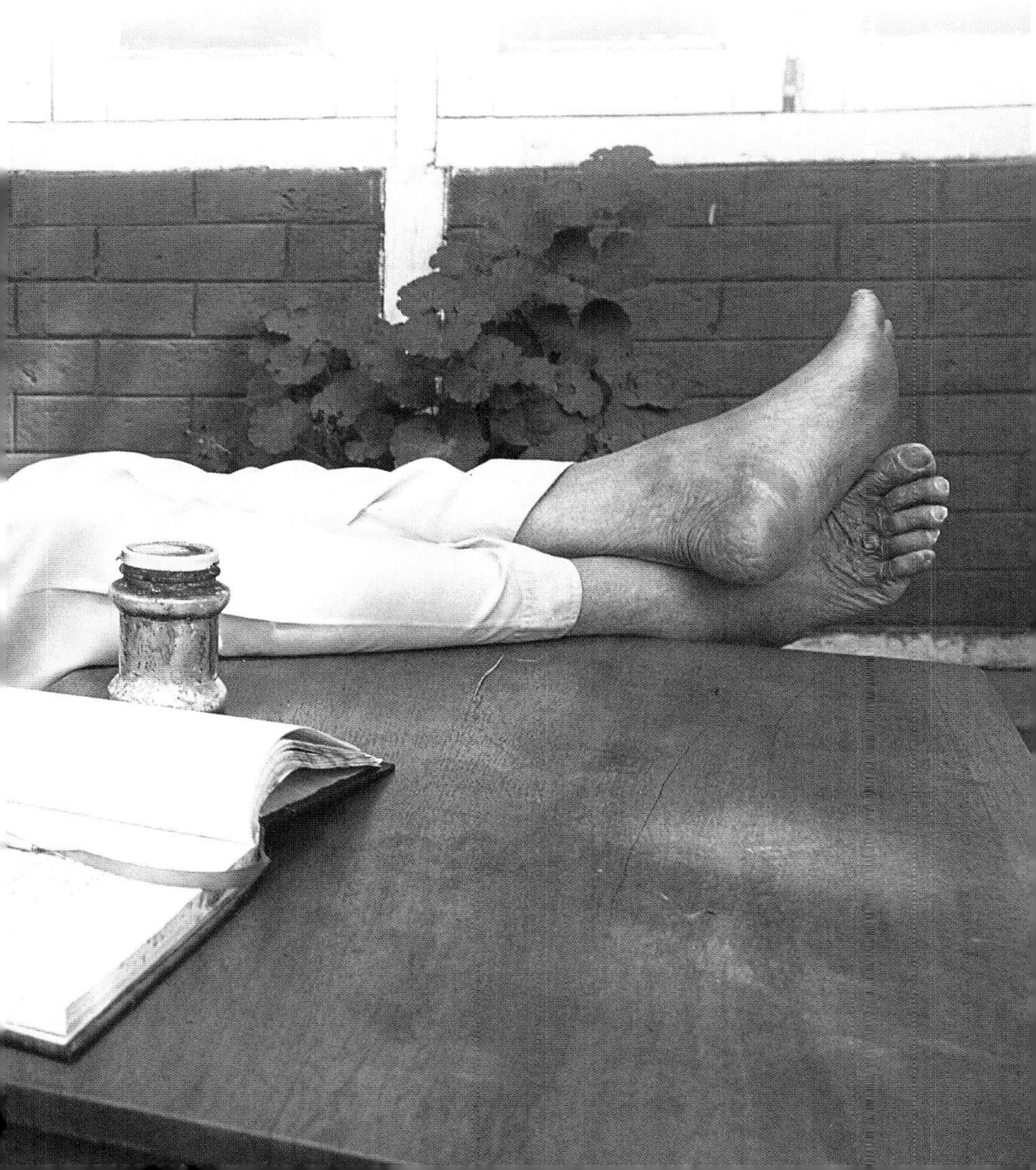

A poem by Rudyard Kipling *If* in many ways sums up the ideals to which my father aspires:

If you can keep your head when all about you
Are losing theirs and blaming it on you,
If you can trust yourself when all men doubt you,
But make allowance for their doubting too,
If you can wait but not be tired by waiting,
Or being lied about, don't deal in lies,
Or being hated, don't give way to hating,
And yet don't look too good, nor talk too wise,

If you can dream—and not make dreams your master,
If you can think—and not make thoughts your aim;
If you can meet with Triumph and Disaster
And treat those two imposters just the same;
If you can bear to hear the truth you've spoken

Twisted by knaves to make a trap for fools,
Or watch the things you gave your life to, broken,
And stoop and build 'em up with worn-out tools,

If you can make one heap of all your winnings
And risk it all on one turn of pitch-and-toss,
And lose, and start again at your beginnings
And never breathe a word about your loss,
If you can force your heart and nerve and sinew
To serve your turn long after they are gone,
And so hold on when there's nothing in you
Except the Will that says to them 'Hold on!'

If you can talk with crowds and keep your virtue
Or walk with kings—nor lose the common touch,
If neither foes nor loving friends can hurt you;
If all men count with you, but none too much,
If you can fill the unforgiving minute
With sixty seconds' worth of distance run,
Yours is the Earth and everything that's in it,
And—which is more—you'll be a Man, my son!'

That is the kind of person my father admires—one who places humanity before a personal quest for salvation.